JUNIOR CYCLE SCIENCE

ESSENTIAL SCiENCE

STUDENT LABORATORY NOTEBOOK

DECLAN KENNEDY
ROSE LAWLOR
SEAN FINN

First published in 2016 by Folens Publishers
Hibernian Industrial Estate, Greenhills Road, Tallaght, Dublin 24

© Declan Kennedy, Rose Lawlor and Sean Finn 2016

Illustrations: Oxford Illustrators and Designers

ISBN 978-1-78090-573-0

To the best of the publisher's knowledge, information in this book was correct at the time of going to press. No responsibility can be taken for any errors.

The FOLENS company name and associated logos are trademarks of Folens Publishers, registered in Ireland and other countries.

The publisher has made every effort to contact all copyright holders but if any have been overlooked, we will be pleased to make any necessary arrangements.

Any links or references to external websites should not be construed as an endorsement by Folens of the content or views of these websites.

Photograph Acknowledgements
Photo on p.12 © iStockphoto. All other photography by John Sexton.

Introduction

This *Student Laboratory Notebook* is designed to help you to keep a record of the laboratory practical work you have carried out as part of the Junior Cycle science course. In this *Laboratory Notebook* you will find detailed step-by-step instructions for carrying out a wide range of experiments described in the *Essential Science* textbook.

Each set of instructions is followed by a detailed Student Write-Up sheet to help you to write a report on the experiment that you have performed. Scientists always have to write reports of their work to help others to understand what they have done. You should complete the report sheet either during the experiment or immediately after it. When you write up the report of the experiment you must begin by writing the **title** of the experiment and the **date** on which you performed the experiment. You will write a list of the **equipment and chemicals** (if any) that you used when carrying out the experiment.

You must then write the main steps to describe what you did to carry out the experiment. This is called the **procedure** of the experiment. When writing up the procedure for each experiment, you need include only the main points. For example, the following report is too detailed: 'I opened a box of filter papers. I took out a filter paper. I folded the filter paper in the shape of a cone. I rinsed a filter funnel with water. I placed a cone of filter paper in it.' Only the last two sentences need be included in your report sheet. These two sentences give all the information that the person reading your account of the experiment requires.

When describing how you carried out the experiment you must always draw a **labelled diagram** of the apparatus you used. It is important that you get into the habit of drawing labelled diagrams. Do not worry if your drawings are not as good as those drawn by professional artists in the textbook. The important point is to ensure that your drawings are clear and well labelled. A well-labelled diagram can save you a lot of writing and also help you to obtain a high mark in an examination. A sentence often used when writing up experiments is 'The apparatus was set up as shown in the diagram.' (The word 'apparatus' means 'laboratory equipment'.)

When you have completed the description of how you carried out the experiment, you must now describe what information you obtained and what you observed during the experiment. This information may be summarised under the heading '**Results and observations**'. In some cases, you may have to summarise your results in the form of a table or a graph or both a table and a graph.

Finally, you will have to describe what you can deduce from the results you obtained and the observations that you made. These are called the **conclusions** of the experiment.

Overall, the write up of each experiment need only fill one page but if you need extra space, a blank page is given at the end of this *Laboratory Notebook,* which you may use to give additional information about the experiment. Your teacher may also give you written questions to test your knowledge and understanding of each experiment. You may keep a record of experiments completed by ticking the box next to each experiment in the Table of Contents.

When carrying out experiments in the laboratory, it is very important that you obey all the Laboratory Safety Rules listed on the inside cover of this *Laboratory Notebook*. Your teacher may give you additional rules.

We hope that you enjoy carrying out these experiments in the laboratory and that they develop your interest in science. They will certainly help you to acquire many practical skills and give you a better understanding of the theoretical parts of the course. We wish you the best of luck!

Declan Kennedy, Rose Lawlor, Sean Finn

Contents

Contents cont.

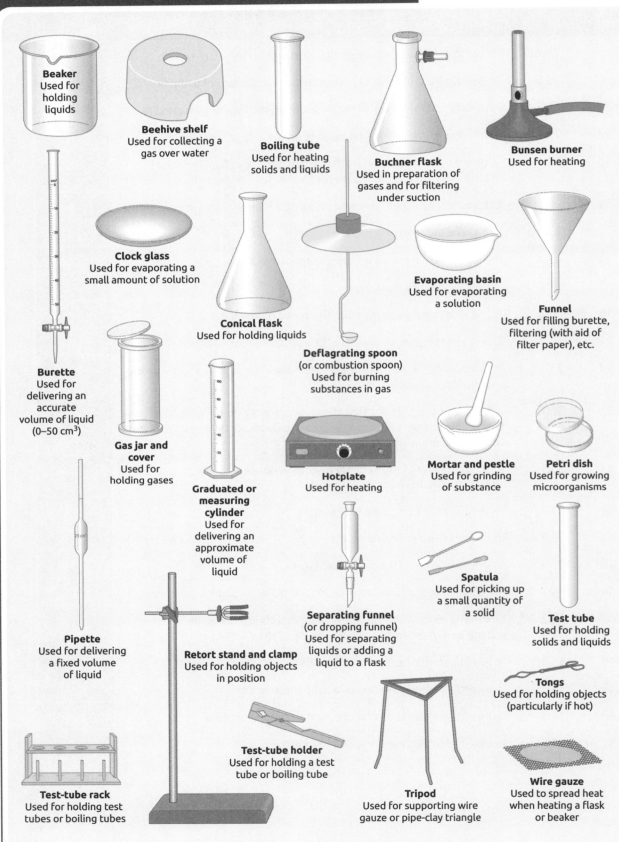

Beaker
Used for holding liquids

Beehive shelf
Used for collecting a gas over water

Boiling tube
Used for heating solids and liquids

Buchner flask
Used in preparation of gases and for filtering under suction

Bunsen burner
Used for heating

Burette
Used for delivering an accurate volume of liquid (0–50 cm³)

Clock glass
Used for evaporating a small amount of solution

Conical flask
Used for holding liquids

Deflagrating spoon
(or combustion spoon)
Used for burning substances in gas

Evaporating basin
Used for evaporating a solution

Funnel
Used for filling burette, filtering (with aid of filter paper), etc.

Gas jar and cover
Used for holding gases

Graduated or measuring cylinder
Used for delivering an approximate volume of liquid

Hotplate
Used for heating

Mortar and pestle
Used for grinding of substance

Petri dish
Used for growing microorganisms

Pipette
Used for delivering a fixed volume of liquid

Retort stand and clamp
Used for holding objects in position

Separating funnel
(or dropping funnel)
Used for separating liquids or adding a liquid to a flask

Spatula
Used for picking up a small quantity of a solid

Test tube
Used for holding solids and liquids

Tongs
Used for holding objects (particularly if hot)

Test-tube holder
Used for holding a test tube or boiling tube

Test-tube rack
Used for holding test tubes or boiling tubes

Tripod
Used for supporting wire gauze or pipe-clay triangle

Wire gauze
Used to spread heat when heating a flask or beaker

Student experiment 1

Experiment 3.1
To use a light microscope

Equipment required: microscope, lens cleaner, prepared slide

Method

Reminder: Keep both eyes open when looking through the microscope.

1. Plug in the microscope and turn the light on.

2. Turn the rotating nosepiece to fix the low-power objective lens in place.

3. While looking through the eyepiece, use the iris diaphragm, under the stage, to adjust the light coming through.

4. Place a slide on the stage.

5. Raise the stage to its highest position.

6. While looking through the eyepiece and using the coarse focus wheel, bring the slide into focus with as clear a view as you can obtain.

7. Now use the fine focus wheel to make the slight adjustment needed to bring the object into clear focus.

8. Observe and draw what you see.

9. Next, rotate the nosepiece to fix the medium-power objective lens in place. ***Only using the fine focus wheel***, bring the object into focus.

10. To view under high power, turn the nosepiece to the highest magnification and ***only*** use the fine focus wheel.

11. Gently wipe the eyepiece and objective lens with the lens cleaner.

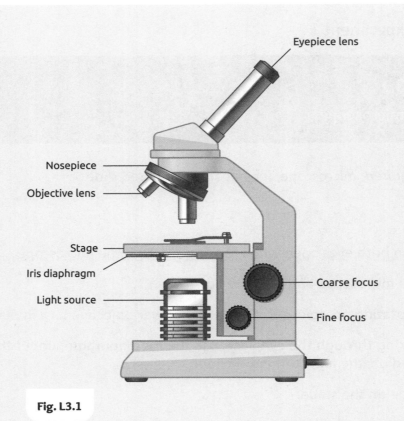

Fig. L3.1

Student write-up

(i) **Title of Experiment 3.1**

To use a light microscope

(ii) **Date** 29/9/2020 **Student** Abdul

(iii) **Equipment used**

Light microscope, Prepared slide

(iv) Procedure (outline what you did)

1. Plug the microscope in and turn the light
2. clip the slide in place on the stage
3. Put the shortest objective over the ~~slide~~ slide
4. look through the eye piece and adjust the focus to get clearer image
5. Make ~~fine~~ small adjasment with the fine focus if necassary
6. Draw what you see, and zoom in by changing the objective

(v) Observations

I saw some ~~Mitochondrian, cells~~ cells and their organells such as nucles and cytoplasm and cell membrane

(vi) Labelled diagram of specimen observed

Questions on this experiment can be found on folensonline.ie.

LABORATORY NOTEBOOK   3

Experiment 3.2

To prepare a glass slide for observation under the microscope

Note: If a stain is used to observe a specimen, iodine is used for plant cells and methylene blue is used for animal cells.

Method

1. Obtain a clean glass slide.

2. Place a very thin layer of the specimen that you wish to observe onto the slide.

3. Place a drop of water (or stain if you are using it) on the specimen.

4. Place a coverslip at a 45° angle to the slide and gently lower it to cover the specimen. This is in order to eliminate air bubbles.

5. Remove any excess liquid using tissue paper.

To obtain a good specimen of plant tissue for viewing under the microscope: onion cells

Equipment required: onion, knife, forceps, glass slide, coverslip, tissue, filter paper, disposable gloves

Chemicals required: water, iodine

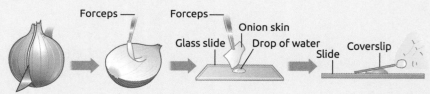

1. Cut down through an onion
2. Use forceps to peel off the inner skin
3. Place onion skin on drop of water
4. Gently lower the coverslip onto the slide

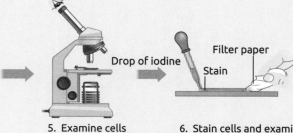

5. Examine cells
6. Stain cells and examine again under microscope

Fig. L3.2

1. Cut an onion lengthwise down the centre.

2. Using one half of the onion and a knife, scoop out the very centre of the onion.

3. Using a pair of tweezers, tear off a layer of the skin that surrounds the fleshy part of the onion. You should obtain a single layer of skin without flesh attached to it. You can obtain more onion skin by scooping out the next layer of flesh.

4. Add iodine stain to the specimen instead of water. The iodine is absorbed by the nucleus of the cell, allowing the nucleus to be clearly visible.

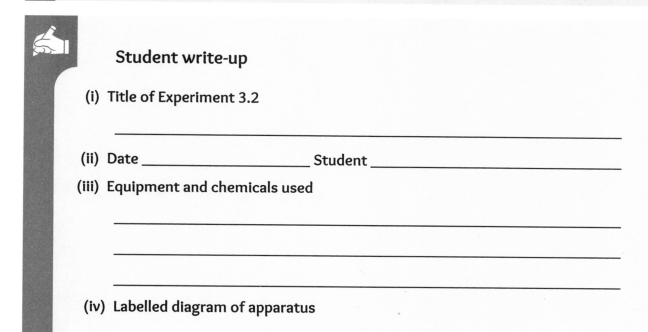

Student write-up

(i) Title of Experiment 3.2

_____

(ii) Date _____ Student _____

(iii) Equipment and chemicals used

_____

_____

_____

(iv) Labelled diagram of apparatus

Questions on this experiment can be found on folensonline.ie.

(v) Procedure (outline what you did)

_____

_____

_____

_____

_____

_____

_____

(vi) Observations

_____

_____

_____

_____

_____

Student experiment 3

Experiment 3.3

To obtain a good specimen of animal tissue for viewing under the microscope: cheek cells

Equipment required: lollipop stick/inoculating loop, glass slide, coverslip, beaker

Chemicals required: water, methylene blue, Milton

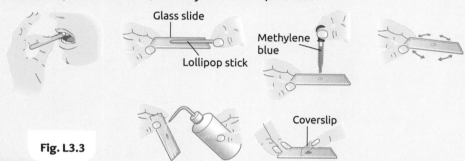

Fig. L3.3

Method

1. Using a clean lollipop stick or a sterile inoculating loop, scrape the inside of your cheek.

2. Rub the stick or loop across a clean glass slide.

3. Be sure not to leave the stick or loop lying around anywhere – it needs to be disposed of by placing in a container with strong bactericide (e.g. Milton). This is to prevent spread of any possible infection.

4. You can add water to the cells, but it is quite difficult to see cheek cells with only water. A stain of methylene blue may be added at this point – to make the cells and nuclei clearly visible.

5. Be sure to dispose of the slide and coverslips in the same manner as the sticks.

Adding methylene blue stain

1. Allow the cheek cells to dry onto the slide by waving it gently in the air.

2. Using a dropper, place one drop of methylene blue on the cheek cells.

3. Gently swivel the slide so that the stain covers the cells.

4. Using a wash bottle over a sink, very gently wash off the methylene blue.

5. Wipe the underside of the slide with tissue.

6. Place a coverslip at a 45° angle to the slide and gently lower it to cover the specimen. This is to avoid air bubbles.

Student write-up

(i) Title of Experiment 3.3

_____

(ii) Date _____ Student _____

(iii) Equipment and chemicals used

_____

(iv) Labelled diagram of apparatus

(v) Procedure (outline what you did)

_____

_____

_____

_____

(vi) Observations

_____

_____

_____

_____

_____

Questions on this experiment can be found on folensonline.ie.

ESSENTIAL SCIENCE

Student experiment 4

Experiment 4.1

To investigate the digestion of starch by amylase

Equipment required: test tubes × 2, test-tube rack, water bath, thermometer, droppers, spotting tile

Chemicals required: starch solution (1% w/v), amylase (1% solution), iodine solution, water

Method

1. Using a dropper, measure out 5 cm³ of the starch solution and add it to a test tube.

2. Repeat step 1.

3. Add 2 cm³ of amylase to one of the test tubes with the starch solution. Label it A.

4. Add 2 cm³ of water to the other test tube with the starch solution. Label it B.

5. Place both test tubes in a water bath at 37 °C for 10 minutes (see Fig. L4.1a).

6. Add 1 cm³ of iodine to two wells of the spotting tile (see Fig. L4.1b).

7. Add 1 cm³ of the starch + water to one of the wells with the iodine.

8. Add 1 cm³ of the starch + amylase to the other well with the iodine.

9. Observe the colours of the iodine.

10. If the iodine turns a blue-black colour in both wells, wait 5 minutes and repeat steps 6–9.

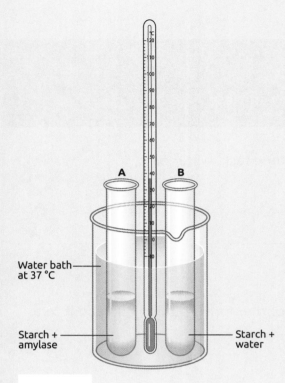

Water bath at 37 °C

Starch + amylase

Starch + water

Fig. L4.1a

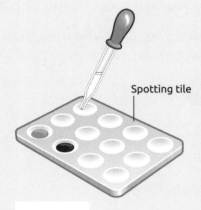

Spotting tile

Fig. L4.1b

Results

	Initial colour of iodine	Final colour of iodine
Starch + water	Orange-brown	
Starch + amylase	Orange-brown	

Student write-up

(i) Title of Experiment 4.1

_____

(ii) Date _____ Student _____

(iii) Equipment and chemicals used

_____

_____

_____

(iv) Procedure (outline what you did)

_____

_____

_____

_____

_____

_____

_____

(v) Results and observations

	Initial colour of iodine	Final colour of iodine
Starch + water	Orange-brown	
Starch + amylase	Orange-brown	

(vi) Labelled diagram of apparatus

(vii) Conclusion

_____

_____

_____

_____

Questions on this experiment may be found on folensonline.ie.

LABORATORY NOTEBOOK   11

Student experiment 5

Experiment 5.1
To investigate the effect of exercise on heart rate

Equipment required: data logger and heart-rate sensor if used, stopwatch

Fig. L5.1

Method

Don't forget to record your results as they happen!

1. Measure the pulse rate while sitting down. This is known as the 'resting rate'.

2. Repeat step 1 twice and get the average pulse rate.

3. Measure the pulse rate while standing.

4. Repeat step 3 twice and get the average pulse rate.

5. Measure the pulse rate after 2 minutes' slow walking.

6. Allow time to return to standing pulse rate.

7. Measure the pulse rate after 2 minutes' fast walking.

8. Allow time to return to standing pulse rate.

9. Measure the pulse rate after 2 minutes' slow running.

10. Allow time to return to standing pulse rate.

11. Measure the pulse rate after 2 minutes' fast running.

12. Allow time to return to standing pulse rate.

Student write-up

(i) Title of Experiment 5.1

_____

(ii) Date _____   Student _____

(iii) Equipment used

_____

_____

_____

(iv) Procedure (outline what you did)

_____

_____

_____

_____

_____

_____

_____

_____

(v) Results and observations

Sitting	
1st pulse rate (bpm)	
2nd pulse rate (bpm)	
3rd pulse rate (bpm)	
Average (bpm)	

Standing	
1st pulse rate (bpm)	
2nd pulse rate (bpm)	
3rd pulse rate (bpm)	
Average (bpm)	

Exercise level	Sitting average	Standing average	Slow walking	Fast walking	Slow running	Fast running
Heart rate/ pulse rate (bpm)						

(vi) Conclusion

_____

_____

_____

_____

_____

Questions on this experiment may be found on folensonline.ie.

14 ESSENTIAL SCIENCE

Student experiment 6

Experiment 6.1
To investigate carbon dioxide in inhaled air and exhaled air

Equipment required: test tubes × 2, glass tubing × 4, two-holed rubber stoppers × 2

Chemicals required: lime water

Method

1. Put the same volume of lime water in two test tubes, labelled A and B.

2. Set up the apparatus as in Fig. L6.1.

3. Suck air in through tube X.

4. Blow air out through tube Y.

5. Keep doing steps 3 and 4 until the lime water in one of the tubes turns milky.

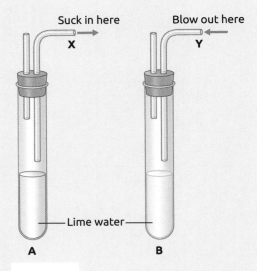

Fig. L6.1

Student write-up

(i) Title of Experiment 6.1

_____

(ii) Date _____   Student _____

(iii) Equipment and chemicals used

_____

_____

_____

(iv) Procedure (outline what you did)

_____

_____

_____

_____

_____

_____

_____

_____

_____

(v) Results and observations

	Test tube A (inhaled air)	Test tube B (exhaled air)
Initial colour of lime water		
Tube in which lime water turned milky first		

(vi) Labelled diagram of apparatus

(vii) Conclusion

_____

_____

_____

_____

_____

Questions on this experiment may be found on folensonline.ie.

18　ESSENTIAL SCIENCE

Experiment 7.1

To investigate how temperature affects respiration

Equipment required: test tubes × 4, balance, graduated cylinder medium, test-tube rack, beakers (water baths) × 4, stirring rod, thermometers × 4, ruler/meter stick, marker/chinagraph pen

Chemicals required: glucose, yeast (1 g), water

Method

1. Place 10 g of glucose in a graduated cylinder. Add water to make 100 ml of solution. Stir well. This is your 10% w/v glucose solution.

2. Add 1 g of yeast to each test tube.

3. Add 20 ml of glucose solution to the yeast and stir well.

4. Mark the level of the liquid in the test tubes with a marker/chinagraph pencil.

5. Place the test tubes in water baths at 10 °C, 20 °C, 30 °C, 40 °C.

6. Wait 6–8 minutes.

7. Measure the depth of foam produced by the yeast in each test tube.

8. Record your results and draw a bar chart of your results.

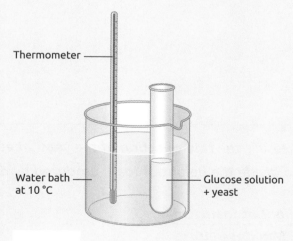

Fig. L7.1

Student write-up

(i) Title of Experiment 7.1

_____

(ii) Date _____   Student _____

(iii) Equipment and chemicals used

_____

(iv) Procedure (outline what you did)

_____

_____

(v) Results and observations

Temperature (°C)	10	20	30	40
Depth of foam (cm)				

(vi) Labelled diagram of apparatus

(vii) Conclusion

_____

How would you measure the rate of action of the yeast at each temperature?

You would need to divide the height of foam produced by the time taken to form the foam, i.e.

$$Rate = \frac{Height\ of\ foam\ (cm)}{Minutes\ (min)} = cm/min$$

Questions on this experiment may be found on folensonline.ie.

20   ESSENTIAL SCIENCE

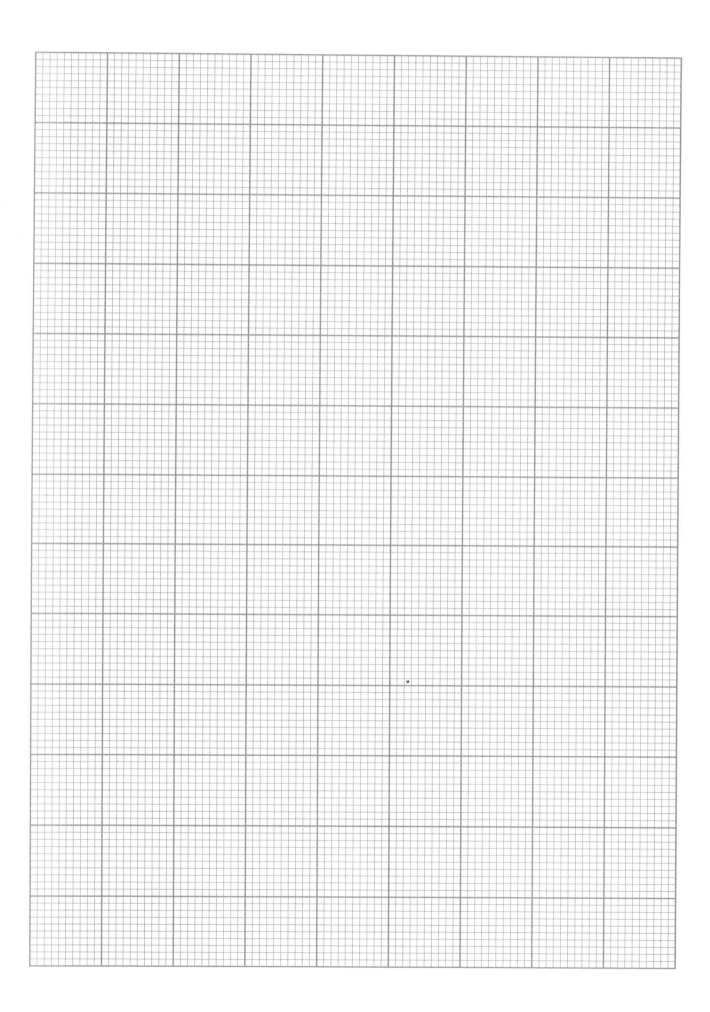

Experiment 8.1

To show that light is necessary for photosynthesis

Equipment required: plant (busy Lizzie, geranium), tinfoil, boiling tubes × 2, water bath, tweezers, test-tube holder, white tile/clock glass

Chemicals required: iodine, methylated spirits/industrial methylated spirit/ethanol

Method

1. Place a plant in a dark place for at least 48 hours. This is to destarch the plant.

2. Remove the plant from the dark and *immediately* cover some of the leaves with tinfoil (see Figure L8.1a).

3. Expose the plant to good sunlight (or a lamp) for 6 hours.

4. Take one covered leaf and one exposed leaf and test both for the presence of starch.

To test a leaf for starch:

1. Put the leaf in hot water to soften it (see Figure L8.1b).

2. Place the leaf in a boiling tube with alcohol (methylated spirits or ethanol).

3. Put the boiling tube with the leaf in a hot water bath (see Figure L8.1c). This is to remove the chlorophyll.

4. Remove the leaf from the boiling tube and wash it in hot water. This is to remove the alcohol and soften the leaf, which will have become brittle.

5. Place the leaf on a white tile and put a little iodine on it (see Figure L8.1d).

6. Record the colour of the iodine.

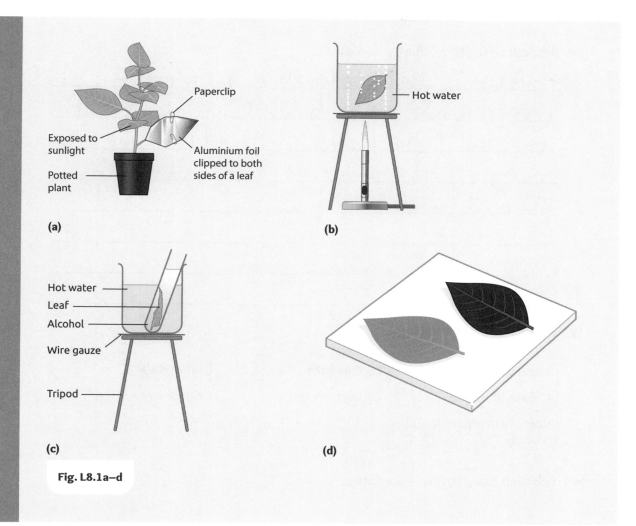

(a)

(b)

(c)

(d)

Fig. L8.1a–d

Student write-up

(i) Title of Experiment 8.1

light needed for photosynthesis

(ii) Date _at / 2021_   Student _Abdul_

(iii) Equipment and chemicals used

Iodine (blue black colour)

(iv) Procedure (outline what you did)

coverd a part of the leaf with paper and leave the plant in light for a feW hours and after testing only the uncovered parts became blue black.

(v) Results and observations

Leaves	Leaf in light	Leaf in dark
Colour of iodine	Orange-brown	Orange-brown
Colour change in iodine (if any)	blue _ black	blue black

(vi) Labelled diagrams of apparatus

(vii) Conclusion

light is needed for Photosynthis

Questions on this experiment may be found on folensonline.ie.

24   ESSENTIAL SCIENCE

Student experiment 9

Experiment 10.1
To extract DNA from kiwi fruit

Equipment required: kiwi, knife, fork, chopping board, electronic balance, graduated cylinder, 10 ml syringe, medium beakers × 2, large beaker, sieve, kitchen paper, wooden skewer, stirring rod

Chemicals required: salt, washing-up liquid, pineapple juice, ice-cold ethanol, water

Method

1. Place 3 g of salt in a medium beaker.

2. Add 80 ml of water and stir well until the salt is dissolved.

3. Using the syringe, add 10 ml of washing-up liquid to the salt solution and stir gently. Try to avoid too many bubbles. This is the extraction solution (see Fig. L10.1).

Fig. L10.1

4. Using the knife, peel the kiwi and chop it into small pieces.

5. Place the chopped kiwi in the second beaker and mash it well with the fork (see Fig. L10.2).

Fig. L10.2

6. Add the extraction solution to the mashed kiwi and allow it to stand at room temperature for 20 minutes (see Fig. L10.3).

7. Place the sieve on top of the large beaker and line it with three sheets of kitchen paper.

8. Pour the kiwi solution gently into the sieve, making sure not to tear the kitchen paper.

Fig. L10.3

9. Press down gently on the kiwi to get the liquid through the sieve (see Fig. L10.4).

10. Transfer the green liquid that is collected in the beaker to half-fill a test tube.

11. Add 1 ml of pineapple juice to the kiwi extract. Pineapple juice contains an enzyme that breaks down the protein that the DNA is wrapped around.

12. Leave it at room temperature for about 5 minutes.

13. Remove the ethanol from the freezer and pour it into the kiwi extract (see Fig. L10.5). You need about the same volume of ethanol as fruit extract.

Fig. L10.4

14. Leave it stand for about 10 minutes.

15. After 10 minutes the DNA will have risen to the top of the ethanol and can be fished out with a wooden skewer (see Fig. L10.5).

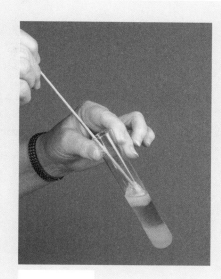

Fig. L10.5

Student write-up

(i) Title of Experiment 10.1

_____

(ii) Date _____ Student _____

(iii) Equipment and chemicals used

_____

_____

_____

(iv) Procedure (outline what you did)

_____

_____

_____

_____

_____

_____

_____

_____

(v) Results and observations

_____

_____

_____

(vi) Labelled diagram of apparatus

(vii) Conclusion

_____

_____

_____

Questions on this experiment may be found on folensonline.ie.

28   ESSENTIAL SCIENCE

Student experiment 10

Experiment 12.1

To test a food sample for starch

Equipment required: small graduated cylinder, test tubes, clock glass, dropper, food samples

Chemicals required: iodine solution

Method

1. If the food sample is a liquid, place 2 cm³ in a test tube.

2. As a control, place 2 cm³ of water in a second test tube.

3. Add 2–3 drops of iodine to each test tube and shake gently.

4. Iodine is orange-brown in colour. Check for any colour change: a blue-black colour indicates the presence of starch; no change in colour indicates the absence of starch.

5. If testing solid food, for example potato, place the food on a clock glass and add the iodine with a dropper.

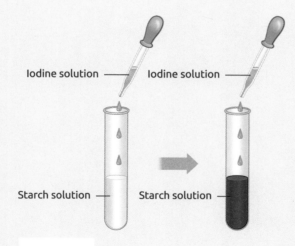

Fig. L12.1

Student write-up

(i) **Title of Experiment 12.1**

_____

(ii) **Date** _____   **Student** _____

(iii) **Equipment and chemicals used**

_____

(iv) **Procedure (outline what you did)**

_____

_____

_____

(v) **Results and observations**

Food			
Colour change			
Starch present			

(vi) **Labelled diagram of apparatus**

(vii) **Conclusion**

_____

_____

Questions on this experiment can be found on folensonline.ie.

30   ESSENTIAL SCIENCE

Experiment 12.2

To test a food sample for glucose

Equipment required: small graduated cylinder, test tubes, clock glass, dropper, hot plate/Bunsen burner (tripod and wire gauze), beaker, pestle and mortar, food samples

Chemicals required: Benedict's solution

Method

1. If the food sample is a liquid, place 2 cm³ in a test tube.

2. As a control, place 2 cm³ of water in a second test tube.

3. Add 2 cm³ of Benedict's solution to each test tube and shake gently.

4. Set up a hot water bath using the hot plate/Bunsen burner.

5. Place the test tubes in the hot water bath for about 5 minutes.

6. Benedict's solution is blue in colour. Check for any colour change: a brick-red colour indicates the presence of glucose; no change in colour indicates the absence of glucose.

7. If testing solid food, for example potato, crush the food with a pestle and mortar and add to some water. Continue as in steps 3–6 above.

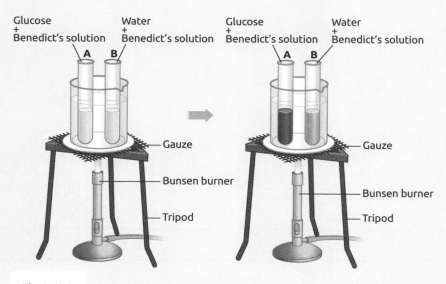

Fig. L12.2

Student write-up

(i) Title of Experiment 12.2

_____

(ii) Date _____ Student _____

(iii) Equipment and chemicals used

_____

_____

(iv) Procedure (outline what you did)

_____

_____

(v) Results and observations

Food			
Colour change			
Glucose present			

(vi) Labelled diagram of apparatus

(vii) Conclusion

_____

_____

Questions on this experiment can be found on folensonline.ie.

Student experiment 12

Experiment 12.3
To test a food sample for protein

Equipment required: small graduated cylinder, test tubes, pestle and mortar, dropper, food samples

Chemicals required: sodium hydroxide solution and copper sulfate solution (biuret solution)

Method

1. If the food sample is a liquid, place 2 cm³ in a test tube.

2. As a control, place 2 cm³ of water in a second test tube.

3. Add 2 cm³ of sodium hydroxide to each test tube.

4. Add 3–4 drops of copper sulfate to each test tube.

5. The test solution is blue in colour: a purple/violet colour indicates the presence of protein; no change in colour indicates the absence of protein.

6. If testing solid food, for example potato, the food needs to be crushed with a pestle and mortar and added to some water. This sample is placed in a test tube and tested as in steps 3–5.

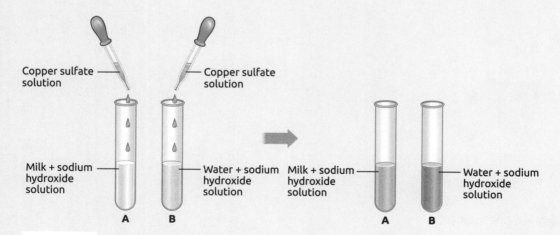

Fig. L12.3

Student write-up

(i) Title of Experiment 12.3

_____

(ii) Date _____ Student _____

(iii) Equipment and chemicals used

_____

_____

(iv) Procedure (outline what you did)

_____

_____

(v) Results and observations

Food			
Colour change			
Protein present			

(vi) Labelled diagram of apparatus

(vii) Conclusion

_____

_____

Questions on this experiment can be found on folensonline.ie.

34   ESSENTIAL SCIENCE

Experiment 12.4

To test a food sample for fat

Equipment required: brown paper, dropper, food samples

Method

1. Place a sample of food on a piece of brown paper.

2. Rub the food into the brown paper and remove any excess food.

3. Wet another piece of brown paper with a little water.

4. Allow both pieces of paper to dry, for about 15 minutes.

5. Examine the brown paper for stains: a permanent translucent stain indicates fat; no stain on the paper indicates that no fat is present.

Note: 'translucent' means that light can pass through it. This is not to be confused with 'transparent', which means that it can be seen through.

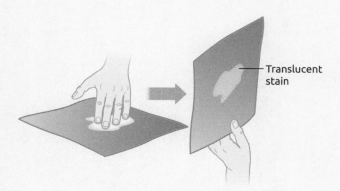

Translucent stain

Fig. L12.4

Student write-up

(i) Title of Experiment 12.4

_____

(ii) Date _____ Student _____

(iii) Equipment used

_____

(iv) Procedure (outline what you did)

_____

_____

(v) Results and observations

Food			
Colour change			
Fat present			

(vi) Labelled diagram of apparatus

(vii) Conclusion

_____

_____

Questions on this experiment may be found on folensonline.ie.

36   ESSENTIAL SCIENCE

Student experiment 14

Experiment 13.1

To show that microorganisms are present in air

Equipment required: sterile agar plates × 2, labels, sticky tape or parafilm, incubator at 20 °C

Method

Tip: Place labels on the underside of the Petri dishes so that they will not obscure your view of the cultures.

1. Take a sterile agar plate, remove the lid and place the lid on the bench (see Fig. L13.1).

2. Leave the open plate exposed to the air for about 10 minutes.

3. Take a second sterile agar plate and do not remove the lid. This is the control.

4. Label the control, and seal the lid with parafilm or tape. This is to ensure that the lids do not fall off after microorganisms grow in them.

5. After the 10-minute exposure, return the lid to the exposed agar plate, label it and seal it.

6. Place both plates upside down in the incubator. This is to prevent condensation from the microorganisms' respiration falling onto the agar.

7. Leave the plates in the incubator for 1 week.

8. After 1 week, check the plates for growth of microorganisms. **Do not open the plates.**

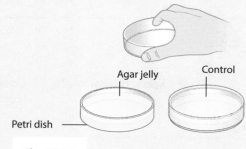

Agar jelly   Control

Petri dish

Fig. L13.1

Safety note:
Your teacher will safely dispose of the Petri dishes by heating them to a very high temperature (120 °C) before placing them in the waste bin. This is to ensure that no disease-causing organisms are on the agar.

Student write-up

(i) Title of Experiment 13.1

____

(ii) Date ________________ Student ________________________

(iii) Equipment used

____

____

____

(iv) Procedure (outline what you did)

____

____

____

____

____

____

____

____

(v) Results and observations

Agar plates	Exposed agar plate	Covered agar plate (control)
Presence of microorganisms		

(vi) Labelled diagram of apparatus

(vii) Conclusion

_____

_____

_____

Questions on this experiment may be found on folensonline.ie.

Student experiment 15

Experiment 14.1
To investigate the frequency of a particular plant species in a habitat

Equipment required: quadrat, clipboard, sheet with grid prepared for recording, pen

Method

1. Choose and identify the plant to be studied.

2. Write the name of the plant in Table L14.1.

3. Taking care to do so safely, throw a pen at random in the habitat to be studied.

4. Place the quadrat where the pen lands.

5. If the chosen plant is in the quadrat, place a tick in the box under quadrat 1. If the plant is not in the quadrat, leave the box blank.

6. Repeat steps 3–5 nine more times.

7. Count how many of the 10 boxes the plant was present in.

8. Write this number under 'Frequency total'.

9. Calculate the percentage incidence of the plant in the 10 quadrat throws. This is the frequency of that plant in the habitat, i.e. the percentage chance of the plant being found in one throw of the quadrat.

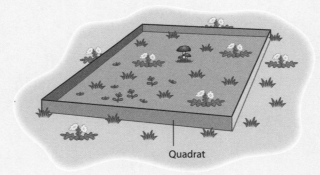

Quadrat

Fig. L14.1

Student write-up

(i) Title of Experiment 14.1

_____

(ii) Date _____ Student _____

(iii) Equipment used

_____

_____

(iv) Procedure (outline what you did)

_____

_____

(v) Results and observations

Plant	Quadrat number										Frequency $= \dfrac{total}{10}$	Percentage frequency
	1	2	3	4	5	6	7	8	9	10		

Table L14.1

(vi) Labelled diagram of apparatus

(vii) Conclusion

_____

Questions on this experiment may be found on folensonline.ie.

LABORATORY NOTEBOOK 41

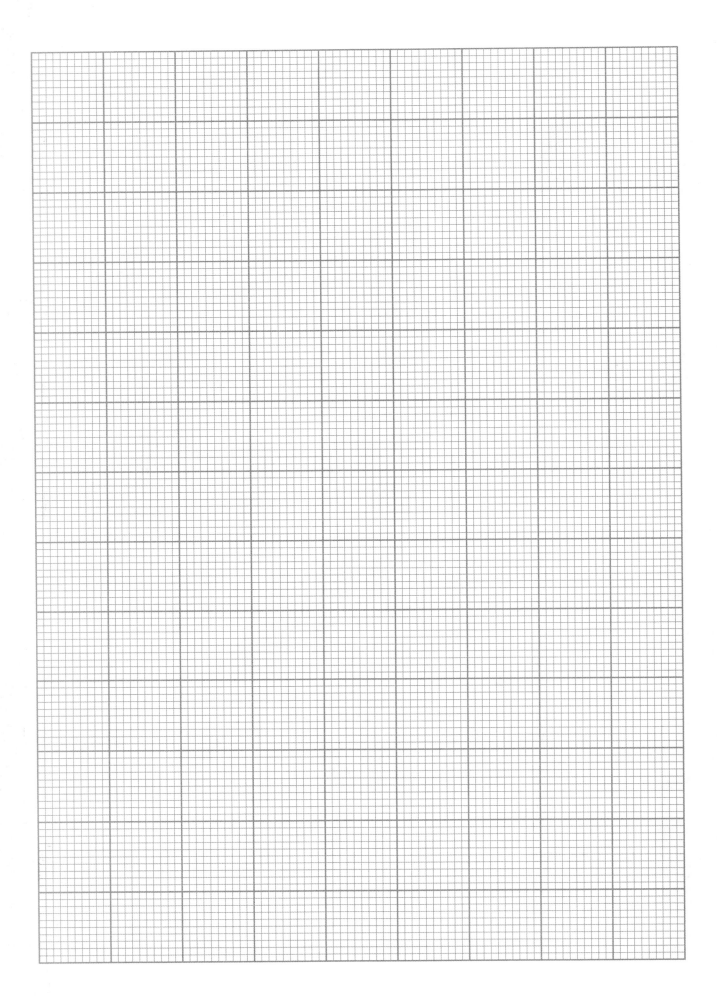

Experiment 16.1

To measure the melting point of benzoic acid

Equipment required: aluminium melting-point block, hotplate, Bunsen burner, melting-point tube, retort stand and boss head, long glass tube or pipe, pestle and mortar, digital thermometer

Chemicals required: benzoic acid

Method

1. Seal the end of a melting-point tube by rotating it for a few seconds in the blue flame of a Bunsen burner.

2. Rotate the open end of the melting-point tube into the sample of benzoic acid crystals (ground up using a pestle and mortar) so that some of the material enters the melting-point tube.

3. Drop the melting-point tube with the sealed end pointing down through a long length of tubing, e.g. glass tubing, standing vertically on the laboratory bench. When the bottom of the melting-point tube hits the laboratory bench, the crystals will fall to the bottom of the melting-point tube. Repeat this procedure until the crystals are at a depth of about 1 cm in the bottom of the melting-point tube.

4. Place the melting-point tube in the aluminium melting-point block on a hotplate (see Fig. L16.1). Insert the probe of a digital thermometer in the aluminium block.

5. Turn on the hotplate and observe the crystals until they melt, i.e. until they change to a colourless liquid.

6. Note the reading on the thermometer at which the crystals melt. This is the melting point of the benzoic acid.

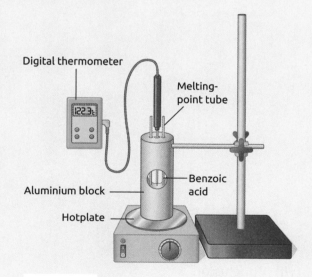

Fig. L16.1

Student write-up

(i) **Title of Experiment 16.1**

_____

(ii) **Date** _____ **Student** _____

(iii) **Equipment and chemicals used**

_____

_____

(iv) **Procedure (outline what you did)**

_____

_____

_____

_____

(v) **Results and observations**

_____

_____

(vi) **Labelled diagram of apparatus**

(vii) **Conclusion**

_____

Questions on this experiment may be found on folensonline.ie.

44   ESSENTIAL SCIENCE

Student experiment 17

Experiment 17.1

To make a mixture using iron and sulfur and then change the mixture into the compound iron sulfide

Introduction

Equipment required: test tube, retort stand and clamp, pestle and mortar, bar magnet, Bunsen burner, cloth, spatula, forceps, hammer (optional), electronic balance, paper, clock glass × 2

Chemicals required: iron filings, sulfur

Method

1. Using the laboratory balance, weigh out on a clock glass 7 g of iron filings.

2. Using another clock glass, weigh out 4 g of sulfur.

3. Mix the 7 g of iron filings and 4 g of sulfur in a pestle and mortar. Grind the mixture very well.

4. Place some of the mixture on a piece of paper. Bring a bar magnet up to the mixture. Write down what you observe.

5. Place some of the mixture in a test tube until it is about one-third full. Clamp the test tube as shown in Fig. L17.1.

6. Using the fume cupboard, heat the bottom of the test tube until the mixture begins to glow. Take away the Bunsen burner at this stage and note that the glow spreads through the material. What can you conclude from this observation?

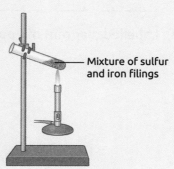

Mixture of sulfur and iron filings

Fig. L17.1

7. Continue heating up along the test tube until the material no longer glows.

8. Allow the test tube to cool. Remove the grey-black material with the assistance of your teacher. Bring a magnet up near the grey material. What do you observe?

Student write-up

(i) **Title of Experiment 17.1**

_____

(ii) **Date** _____ **Student** _____

(iii) **Equipment and chemicals used**

_____

(iv) **Procedure (outline what you did)**

_____

_____

_____

_____

(v) **Results and observations**

_____

_____

(vi) **Conclusions**

_____

(vii) **Labelled diagram of apparatus**

Questions on this experiment may be found on folensonline.ie.

ESSENTIAL SCIENCE

Student experiment 18

Experiment 18.1
To grow crystals of copper sulfate

Equipment required: pestle and mortar, stirring rod, beaker, hotplate/ Bunsen burner (tripod and wire gauze), evaporating basin, thermometer, spatula

Chemicals required: alum or copper sulfate, water

Method

1. Grind up a sample of copper sulfate using a pestle and mortar.

2. Use the spatula to gradually add the powdered substance to 100 cm³ of water in a beaker, as shown in Figure L18.1. Use a stirring rod to stir the solution after each addition, as stirring helps the powder to dissolve more quickly. Continue adding until the solute no longer dissolves but settles at the bottom of the beaker.

3. Using a thermometer, note the temperature of the water.

4. Heat the water to about 60 °C and note that the undissolved copper sulfate now dissolves.

5. Add in more copper sulfate and heat until no more will dissolve.

6. Pour about half of the solution into a warm evaporating basin and put it aside to cool slowly.

7. Cool the other half quickly by holding the beaker under running water from the tap.

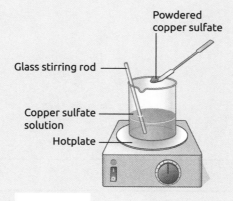

Powdered copper sulfate

Glass stirring rod

Copper sulfate solution

Hotplate

Fig. L18.1

Student write-up

(i) **Title of Experiment 18.1**

_____

(ii) **Date** _____ **Student** _____

(iii) **Equipment and chemicals used**

_____

_____

(iv) **Procedure (outline what you did)**

_____

_____

(v) **Results and observations**

_____

_____

(vi) **Labelled diagram of apparatus**

(vii) **Conclusion**

_____

_____

Questions on this experiment may be found on folensonline.ie.

Student experiment 19

Experiment 18.2

To investigate the effect of temperature on solubility and to use the data obtained to plot a solubility curve

Equipment required: beaker, thermometer, stirring rod, hotplate/ Bunsen burner (tripod and wire gauze), spatula, pestle and mortar, electronic balance

Chemicals required: copper sulfate (or any substance that dissolves in water), water

Method

1. Grind up a sample of the substance (e.g. copper sulfate) with a pestle and mortar.

2. Weigh out 100 g of the powdered substance.

3. Place 100 cm³ of water in a beaker and heat the water to about 30 °C.

4. Measure the exact temperature of the water using a thermometer.

5. Add some of the copper sulfate using the spatula and stir after each addition (see Fig. L18.2).

6. Continue adding the copper sulfate until no more will dissolve, i.e. until a few grains of the salt remain undissolved at the bottom of the beaker.

7. Weigh the amount of copper sulfate that you have **not** added to the water.

8. By subtraction, calculate the amount of the copper sulfate that has dissolved in the water.

9. Repeat the experiment at various other temperatures.

10. Summarise your results in a table and also by means of a graph on graph paper.

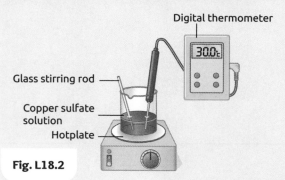

Fig. L18.2

Student write-up

(i) Title of Experiment 18.2

_____

(ii) Date _____   Student _____

(iii) Equipment and chemicals used

_____

(iv) Procedure (outline what you did)

_____

_____

_____

(v) Results and observations

Temperature (°C)	Solubility, i.e. mass of copper sulfate (g) that will dissolve in 100 g of water

(vi) Labelled diagram of apparatus

(vii) Conclusion

_____

Questions on this experiment may be found on folensonline.ie.

50   ESSENTIAL SCIENCE

Experiment 19.1

To separate a mixture of water and soil using filtration

Equipment required: filter paper, filter funnel, glass rod, retort stand and clamp, wash bottle, beaker, conical flask

Chemicals required: mixture of water and soil

Method

1. Take a filter paper and fold it into the shape of a cone as shown by your teacher.

2. Rinse a filter funnel with water and place the cone of filter paper in it, as shown in Fig. L19.1. Rinsing the filter funnel not only cleans it but also helps the filter paper to stick to it.

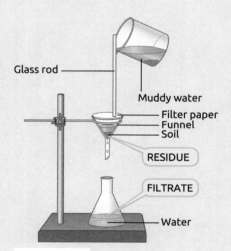

Glass rod

Muddy water

Filter paper
Funnel
Soil

RESIDUE

FILTRATE

Water

Fig. L19.1

3. Set up the apparatus shown in Fig. L19.1. Carefully pour some of the mixture down a glass rod and into the filter funnel. The purpose of the glass rod is to prevent any splashing and to make sure that the mixture does not get between the paper and the funnel. Do not allow the glass rod to touch against the filter paper, as it may tear it.

4. Keep adding the mixture until it has all been filtered.

5. Open the filter paper and allow the soil to dry. This may be done by leaving it to air-dry overnight. Alternatively, the filter paper may be placed on a wire gauze on a hotplate.

Student write-up

(i) Title of Experiment 19.1

_____

(ii) Date _____   Student _____

(iii) Equipment and chemicals used

_____

_____

(iv) Procedure (outline what you did)

_____

_____

_____

_____

_____

_____

(v) Results and observations

_____

_____

(vi) Labelled diagram of apparatus

(vii) Conclusion

_____

_____

Questions on this experiment may be found on folensonline.ie.

Experiment 19.2

To separate sodium chloride from a solution of sodium chloride in water

Equipment required: evaporating basin, hotplate, tongs

Chemicals required: salt solution

Method

1. Pour the salt solution into an evaporating basin. Place the evaporating basin on a hotplate, as shown in Fig. L19.2.

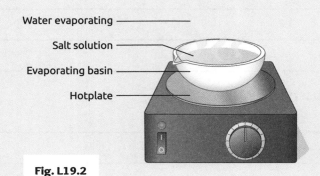

Water evaporating ——————————

Salt solution ——————

Evaporating basin ——————

Hotplate ——————

Fig. L19.2

2. Heat the evaporating basin gently until most of the water has evaporated. It is very important that you wear your safety glasses when evaporating the solution, as the solution can 'spit'. If this occurs, turn down the heat control on the hotplate.

3. Continue heating the evaporating basin until almost all of the water has evaporated. Then adjust the heat control on the hotplate so that the evaporating basin is very gently heated until all of the water is gone. Alternatively, the remaining water may be allowed to evaporate overnight. Use a tongs when removing the evaporating basin from the hotplate, as the evaporating basin may be very hot.

4. Carefully remove the salt from the evaporating basin and show it to your teacher.

Student write-up

(i) **Title of Experiment 19.2**

_____

(ii) **Date** _____ **Student** _____

(iii) **Equipment and chemicals used**

_____

_____

(iv) **Procedure (outline what you did)**

_____

_____

_____

_____

(v) **Results and observations**

_____

_____

(vi) **Labelled diagram of apparatus**

(vii) **Conclusion**

_____

_____

Questions on this experiment may be found on folensonline.ie.

Experiment 19.3

To separate salt from rock salt using filtration and evaporation

Equipment required: pestle and mortar, beaker, stirring rod, hotplate, conical flask, evaporating basin, wash bottle, retort stand and clamp, filter funnel, filter paper

Chemicals required: rock salt

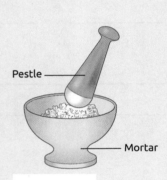

Pestle

Mortar

Fig. L19.3a

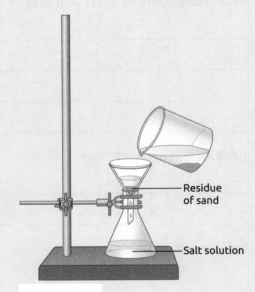

Residue of sand

Salt solution

Fig. L19.3b

Method

1. Crush some small lumps of rock salt using a pestle and mortar, as shown in Fig. L19.3a. Do not forget to wear your safety glasses.

2. Place the rock salt in a beaker of warm water and stir to dissolve the salt. Add more water, if necessary, to dissolve all the salt and continue heating over the hotplate for about 15 minutes.

3. Turn off the hotplate and leave the beaker to stand until it has cooled down. Filter the warm mixture into a conical flask or an evaporating basin, as shown in Fig. L19.3b.

4. Evaporate the water from the sodium chloride solution using the method described in Experiment 19.2. Examine what is left in the evaporating basin.

Student write-up

(i) Title of Experiment 19.3

_____

(ii) Date _____ Student _____

(iii) Equipment and chemicals used

_____

_____

(iv) Procedure (outline what you did)

_____

_____

_____

(v) Results and observations

_____

_____

(vi) Labelled diagram of apparatus

(vii) Conclusion

_____

_____

Questions on this experiment may be found on folensonline.ie.

Student experiment 23

Experiment 19.4

To obtain a sample of pure water from sea water

Equipment required: beakers, retort stands and clamps x 2, tripod, wire gauze, Bunsen burner, conical flask, rubber tubing, Quickfit apparatus (27BU) – Liebig condenser, thermometer, pear-shaped flask, receiver adaptor, still head

Chemicals required: sea water or salt water, anti-bumping granules

Method

1. Pour about 50 cm³ of sea water into the distillation flask. Add a few anti-bumping granules to the sea water (these help the liquid to boil more smoothly). Set up the apparatus shown in Fig. L19.4.

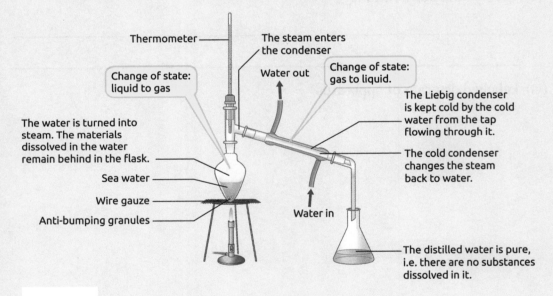

Thermometer

The steam enters the condenser

Change of state: liquid to gas

Water out

Change of state: gas to liquid.

The Liebig condenser is kept cold by the cold water from the tap flowing through it.

The water is turned into steam. The materials dissolved in the water remain behind in the flask.

The cold condenser changes the steam back to water.

Sea water

Wire gauze

Anti-bumping granules

Water in

The distilled water is pure, i.e. there are no substances dissolved in it.

Fig. L19.4

2. Turn on the water to the Liebig condenser. Examine the condenser and note that it is simply a narrow tube surrounded by an outer tube through which water flows. The purpose of the water is to keep the inner tube cool.

3. Heat the distillation flask gently to obtain steady boiling. When the liquid is boiling steadily, read the temperature on the thermometer. Write down what you observe happening in the conical flask.

4. Remove the Bunsen burner when most of the liquid has been boiled off.

Student write-up

(i) **Title of Experiment 19.4**

_____

(ii) **Date** _____ **Student** _____

(iii) **Equipment and chemicals used**

_____

_____

(iv) **Procedure (outline what you did)**

_____

_____

_____

(v) **Results and observations**

_____

_____

(vi) **Labelled diagram of apparatus**

(vii) **Conclusion**

_____

_____

Questions on this experiment may be found on folensonline.ie.

Student experiment 24

Experiment 19.5

To separate the dyes in a sample of ink using chromatography

Equipment required: gas jar, glass rod, dropper, strip of filter paper or chromatography paper, scissors, paperclip, pencil

Chemicals required: markers of various colours (black, brown, etc.), water (if the dye is water soluble), propanone, ethanol, cyclohexane, etc. if the dye is not water soluble

Method

1. Cut a strip of absorbent paper (filter paper or chromatography paper or from the side of a newspaper) long enough for a gas jar, as shown in Fig. L19.5.

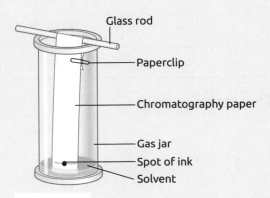

Glass rod

Paperclip

Chromatography paper

Gas jar
Spot of ink
Solvent

Fig. L19.5

2. Using a pencil, draw a line about 3 cm from the end of the paper to indicate where the spot will be placed.

3. Using a marker, place a spot of ink on the line. If the dye is in liquid form, use a dropper to put a spot of ink on the paper. Using the pencil, write the colour of the ink and solvent on the top of the paper. (Your teacher will tell you what solvent to use.)

4. Pour some solvent into the container to a depth of 2 cm maximum and hang the paper so that the solvent level is below the ink mark, as shown in Fig. L19.5.

5. When the solvent reaches the top of the paper, take out the paper and allow it to dry. Examine the chromatogram and note the colours of the dyes that were in the ink.

6. Repeat the experiment using a different colour of ink.

Student write-up

(i) **Title of Experiment 19.5**

_____

(ii) **Date** _____ **Student** _____

(iii) **Equipment and chemicals used**

_____

_____

(iv) **Procedure (outline what you did)**

_____

_____

_____

_____

(v) **Results and observations**

_____

_____

(vi) **Labelled diagram of apparatus**

(vii) **Conclusion**

_____

_____

Questions on this experiment may be found on folensonline.ie.

Experiment 20.1

To investigate the pH of a variety of materials

Equipment required: rack of test tubes, universal indicator paper 1–14 and various narrow-range indicator papers

Chemicals required: dilute hydrochloric acid, dilute sodium hydroxide solution, vinegar, sodium carbonate, lime water, washing soda, tea, milk, detergent, baking powder, indigestion powder, orange juice, lemon juice, oven cleaner, toothpaste, lemonade, cola, acid drops, ammonia solution, rain water, etc.

Method

1. Use a wide-range universal indicator paper (1–14) to find the approximate pH value of each solution. The substances tested may be taken from the above list of chemicals. If the substance is a solid, dissolve it in water before you test it. Match the colour obtained against the colour chart that comes with the paper.

2. Choose a suitable narrow-range paper and measure each pH value more accurately. Again, this is done by matching the colour obtained against the colour chart that comes with the paper.

3. Summarise your results in the form of a number line, as shown in Fig. L20.1. Show the pH of the substance you have tested on the number line.

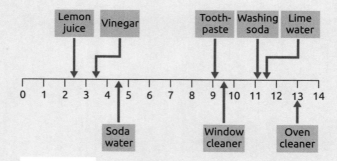

Fig. L20.1

Student write-up

(i) **Title of Experiment 20.1**

to invistigute the Ph of variety of materials

(ii) **Date** 20/6/21   **Student** Abby

(iii) **Equipment and chemicals used**

Acids, Qases

(iv) **Procedure (outline what you did)**

used ~~red~~ and blue unevirsal indecator
palar ~~~~ to check if it's a base
or acid

(v) **Results and observations**

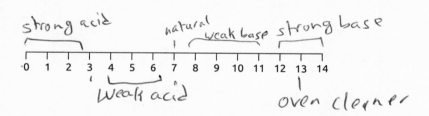

strong acid   natural   weak base   strong base

0 1 2 3 4 5 6 7 8 9 10 11 12 13 14

weak acid

oven cleaner

(vi) **Labelled diagram of apparatus**

(vii) **Conclusion**

Questions on this experiment may be found on folensonline.ie.

LABORATORY NOTEBOOK   63

Experiment 21.1

To investigate if mass is unchanged when a physical change takes place

Equipment required: plastic container with lid, electronic balance

Chemicals required: ice cubes

Method

1. Place some ice cubes in a plastic container.

2. Place the lid on the container.

3. Place the container, lid and contents on an electronic balance, as shown in Fig. L21.1.

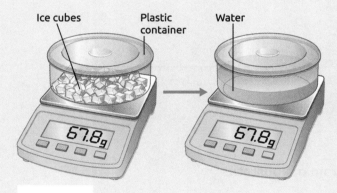

Fig. L21.1

4. Note the reading on the electronic balance.

5. Allow the ice cubes to melt.

6. Note the reading on the electronic balance.

Student write-up

(i) Title of Experiment 21.1

_____

(ii) Date _____ **Student** _____

(iii) Equipment and chemicals used

_____

_____

(iv) Procedure (outline what you did)

_____

_____

_____

_____

(v) Results and observations

_____

_____

(vi) Labelled diagram of apparatus

(vii) Conclusion

_____

Questions on this experiment may be found on folensonline.ie.

LABORATORY NOTEBOOK 65

Student experiment 27

Experiment 21.2

To investigate if mass is unchanged when a chemical reaction takes place

Equipment required: conical flask, small test tube, electronic balance, thread or light string, rubber stopper

Chemicals required: sodium chloride solution (0.1 M), silver nitrate solution (0.1 M)

Method

1. Pour about 20 cm³ of sodium chloride solution into a conical flask.

2. Fill a small test tube to about half its capacity with some silver nitrate solution.

3. Tie a piece of thread around the mouth of the small test tube. Carefully lower the test tube into the conical flask to avoid mixing the two solutions.

4. Place a rubber bung on the conical flask and place the apparatus on an electronic balance, as shown in Fig. L21.2.

Sodium chloride solution   Thread

Silver nitrate solution

Fig. L21.2

5. Note the reading on the electronic balance.

6. Shake the conical flask so that the two solutions mix with each other.

7. Write down your observation.

8. Place the conical flask on the electronic balance.

9. Write down your observation.

Student write-up

(i) Title of Experiment 21.2

_____

(ii) Date _____ **Student** _____

(iii) Equipment and chemicals used

_____

_____

(iv) Procedure (outline what you did)

_____

_____

_____

_____

(v) Results and observations

_____

_____

(vi) Labelled diagram of apparatus

(vii) Conclusion

_____

Questions on experiments 21.1 and 21.2 may be found on folensonline.ie.

Experiment 21.3

To investigate the effect of types of reactants on the rate of a reaction

IMPORTANT SAFETY NOTICE

Hydrogen gas is extremely flammable and forms an explosive mixture with air. No naked flames should be in use in the laboratory.

Equipment required: conical flask, one-hole rubber stopper, glass tubing, rubber tubing, plastic graduated cylinder, retort stand and clamp, stopclock, glass trough or plastic basin

Chemicals required: magnesium ribbon, granulated zinc, hydrochloric acid (1 M)

Method

1. Using a graduated cylinder, place 50 cm³ of 1 M hydrochloric acid in a conical flask.

2. Obtain 6 cm of magnesium ribbon from your teacher.
   (This has a mass of approximately 0.07 g.)

3. Set up the apparatus shown in Fig. L21.3. Use a 100 cm³ graduated cylinder to collect the hydrogen gas.

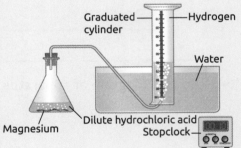

Fig. L21.3

4. Add the magnesium metal to the acid, and immediately place the stopper on the flask and start the stopclock. Give the conical flask a brief, gentle shake.

5. At regular intervals (e.g. every 10 seconds) record the volume of hydrogen given off in Table L21.1. If you find it difficult to read the graduations on the plastic graduated cylinder, place a dark sheet of paper behind it.

6. When the reaction is over, note the final volume of hydrogen collected, and then wash out the conical flask.

7. Repeat the experiment using 5 g of zinc metal instead of magnesium metal. (The increased quantity of zinc is necessary in order to give some evidence of a gas being formed.)

8. Record your results in Table L21.2.

9. Using graph paper, plot a graph of volume of hydrogen (y-axis) against time (x-axis) for each of the two experiments.

Student write-up

(i) Title of Experiment 21.3

_____

(ii) Date _____   Student _____

(iii) Equipment and chemicals used

_____

(iv) Procedure (outline what you did)

_____

_____

(v) Results and observations

Time (s)									
Volume of H_2 (cm³)									

Table L21.1 Reaction of magnesium and hydrochloric acid

Time (s)									
Volume of H_2 (cm³)									

Table L21.2 Reaction of zinc and hydrochloric acid

_____

(vi) Labelled diagram of apparatus

(vii) Conclusion

_____

Questions on this experiment can be found on folensonline.ie.

LABORATORY NOTEBOOK   69

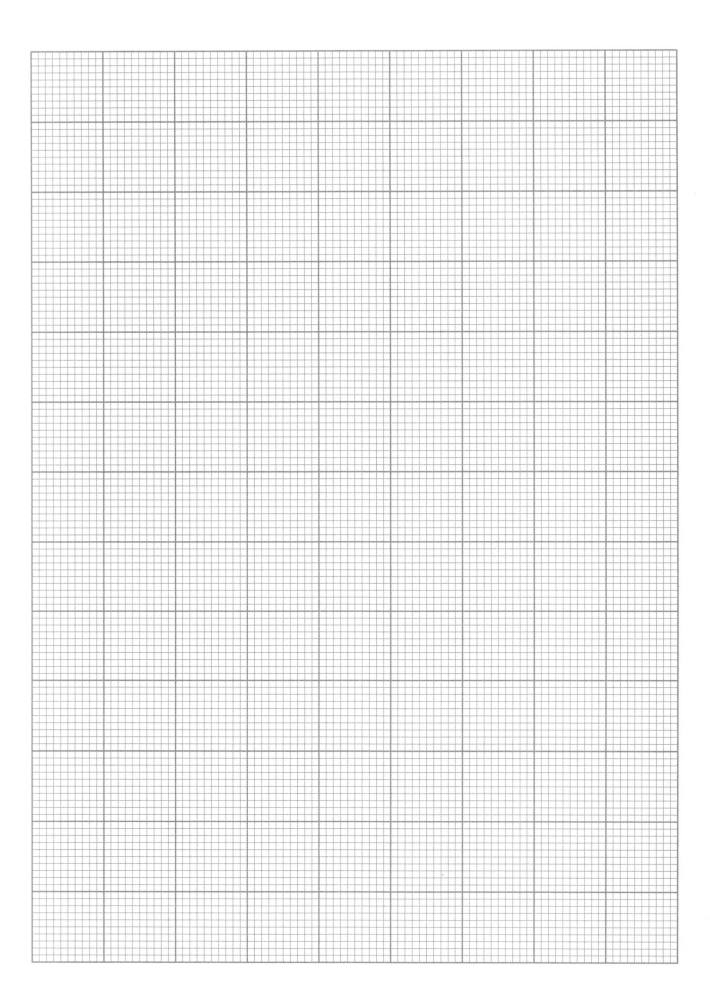

Experiment 21.4

To investigate the effect of particle size on the rate of a reaction

Equipment required: conical flask, graduated cylinder, stopclock, electronic balance, cotton wool

Chemicals required: marble chips, hydrochloric acid (3 M)

Method

1. Place a conical flask containing about 20 g of large marble chips on the pan of an electronic balance, as shown in Fig. L21.4.

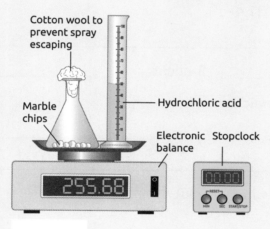

Fig. L21.4

2. Also place a piece of cotton wool and a graduated cylinder containing about 50 cm³ of dilute hydrochloric acid on the pan of the electronic balance.

3. Note the total mass of the conical flask, marble chips, cotton wool, graduated cylinder and hydrochloric acid. Enter the result in Table L21.3.

4. Add the acid to the conical flask containing the marble chips. Swirl the flask to help mix the two chemicals. Insert the cotton wool plug in the mouth of the conical flask and immediately start the stopclock.

5. Place the conical flask and the empty graduated cylinder on the pan of the electronic balance.

6. Note the reading on the electronic balance every 30 seconds.

7. Record the data in Table L21.3.

8. Calculate the loss in mass by subtracting each value of the mass at a particular time from the mass before the acid was added to the marble, i.e. loss in mass at a given time = mass at start – mass at that time.

9. Repeat the experiment with the same mass of medium-sized marble chips.

10. Repeat the experiment with the same mass of very small marble chips.

11. Using graph paper, plot a graph of total mass in grams (y-axis) against time in minutes (x-axis) for each experiment.

12. Using graph paper, plot a graph of loss of mass in grams (y-axis) against time in minutes (x-axis) for each experiment.

Student write-up

(i) Title of Experiment 21.4

_____

(ii) Date _____   Student _____

(iii) Equipment and chemicals used

_____

_____

(iv) Procedure (outline what you did)

_____

_____

_____

_____

_____

_____

_____

_____

_____

_____

_____

_____

Results

Large marble chips

Time (min)								
Total mass (g)								
Loss in mass (g)								

Medium-sized marble chips

Time (min)								
Total mass (g)								
Loss in mass (g)								

Small marble chips

Time (min)								
Total mass (g)								
Loss in mass (g)								

Table L21.3

(vi) Observations

_____

_____

_____

(vii) Labelled diagram of apparatus

(viii) Conclusion

_____

_____

Questions on this experiment may be found on folensonline.ie.

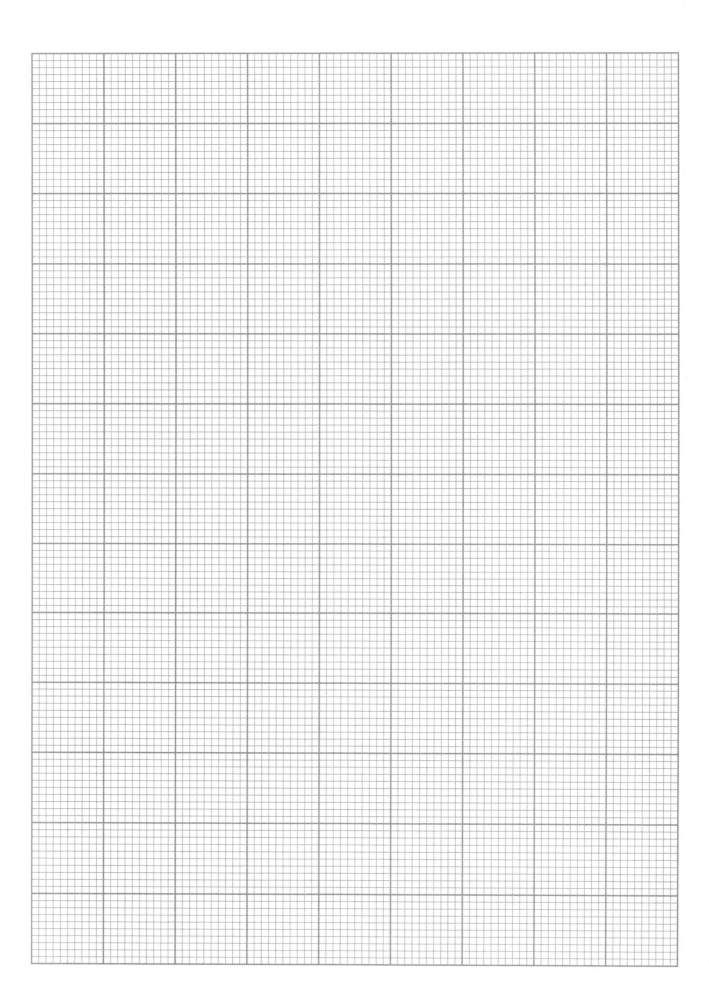

Student experiment 30

Experiment 21.5

To investigate the effect of concentration on the rate of a reaction

IMPORTANT SAFETY NOTICE

Hydrogen gas is extremely flammable and forms an explosive mixture with air. No naked flames should be in use in the laboratory.

Equipment required: conical flask, one-hole rubber stopper, glass tubing, rubber tubing, plastic graduated cylinder, retort stand and clamp, stopclock, glass trough or plastic basin

Chemicals required: magnesium ribbon, hydrochloric acid (0.5 M, 1 M and 1.5 M)

Method

1. Using a graduated cylinder, place 50 cm³ of 0.5 M hydrochloric acid in a conical flask.

2. Obtain 6 cm of magnesium ribbon from your teacher. (This has a mass of approximately 0.07 g.)

3. Set up the apparatus shown in Fig. L21.5. Use a 100 cm³ graduated cylinder to collect the hydrogen gas.

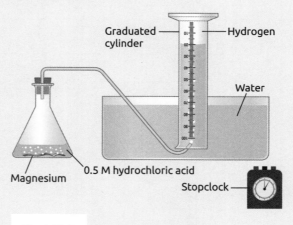

Fig. L21.5

4. Add the magnesium metal to the acid, and immediately place the stopper on the flask and start the stopclock. Give the conical flask a brief, gentle shake.

5. At regular intervals (e.g. every 30 seconds) record in Table L21.4 the volume of hydrogen given off.

6. When the reaction is over, note the final volume of hydrogen collected, and then wash out the conical flask.

7. Repeat the experiment using the same mass of magnesium metal but use 1 M hydrochloric acid (i.e. use acid with twice the concentration of the original acid).

8. When the reaction is over, note the final volume of hydrogen collected, and then wash out the conical flask.

9. Repeat the experiment using the same mass of magnesium metal but use 1.5 M hydrochloric acid (i.e. use acid with three times the concentration of the original acid).

10. When the reaction is over, note the final volume of hydrogen collected, and then wash out the conical flask.

11. On the same sheet of graph paper, plot a graph of volume of hydrogen (y-axis) against time (x-axis) for each of the three concentrations of acid.

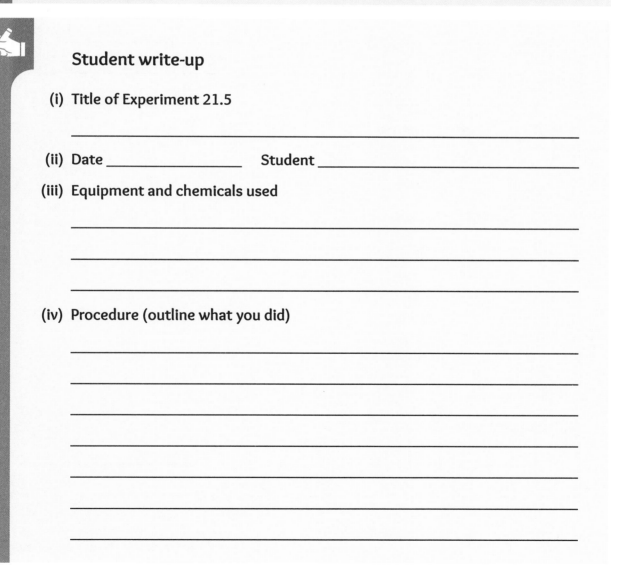

Student write-up

(i) Title of Experiment 21.5

_____

(ii) Date _____   Student _____

(iii) Equipment and chemicals used

_____

_____

_____

(iv) Procedure (outline what you did)

_____

_____

_____

_____

_____

_____

_____

_____

(v) Results

Time (min)													
Volume of H_2 (cm³) using 0.5 M HCl													
Volume of H_2 (cm³) using 1 M HCl													
Volume of H_2 (cm³) using 1.5 M HCl													

Table L21.4

(vi) Observations

_____

_____

_____

_____

_____

_____

(vii) Labelled diagram of apparatus

(viii) Conclusions

_____

_____

Questions on this experiment can be found on folensonline.ie.

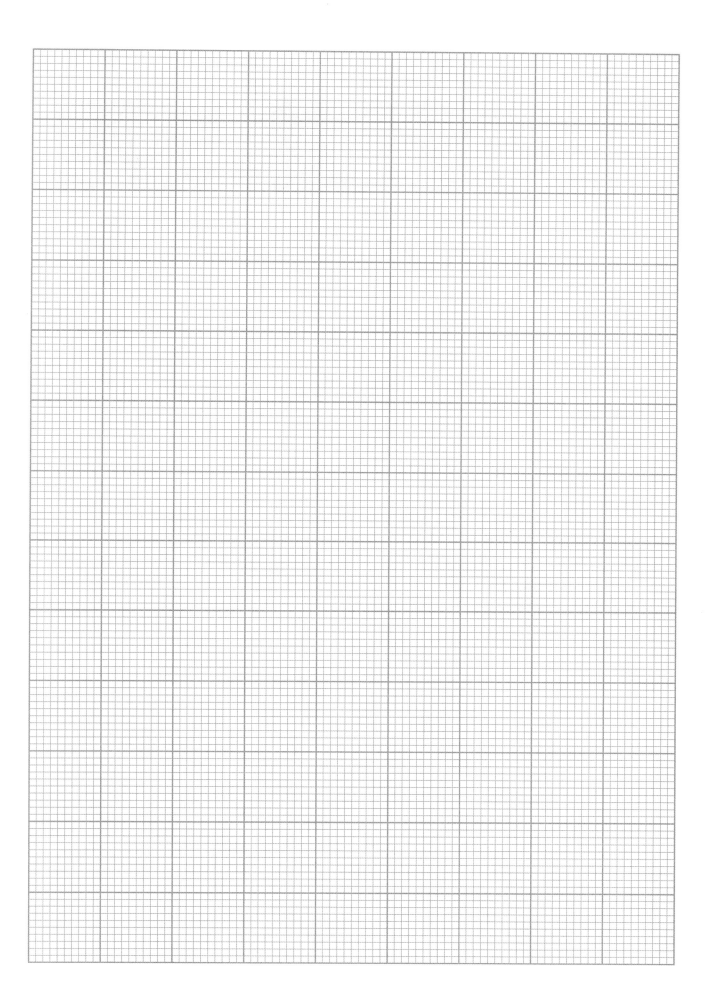

Experiment 21.6

To investigate the effect of temperature on the rate of a reaction

IMPORTANT SAFETY NOTICE

Hydrogen gas is extremely flammable and forms an explosive mixture with air. No naked flames should be in use in the laboratory.

Equipment required: conical flask, one-hole rubber stopper, glass tubing, rubber tubing, graduated cylinder, retort stand and clamp, stopclock, glass trough or plastic basin, digital thermometer, hotplate

Chemicals required: magnesium ribbon, hydrochloric acid (0.5 M)

Method

1. Using a graduated cylinder, place 50 cm³ of 0.5 M hydrochloric acid in a conical flask.

2. Use a thermometer to measure the temperature of the hydrochloric acid and note it down.

3. Obtain 6 cm of magnesium ribbon from your teacher. (This has a mass of approximately 0.07 g.)

4. Set up the apparatus shown in Fig. L21.6. Use a 100 cm³ graduated cylinder to collect the hydrogen gas.

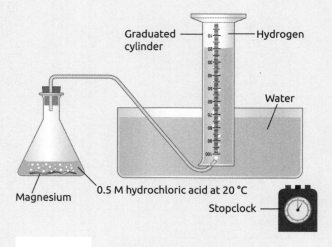

Fig. L21.6

5. Add the magnesium metal to the acid, and immediately place the stopper on the flask and start the stopclock. Give the conical flask a brief, gentle shake.

6. At regular intervals (e.g. every 10 seconds) record in Table L21.5 the volume of hydrogen given off.

7. When the reaction is over, note the final volume of hydrogen collected, and then wash out the conical flask.

8. Repeat the experiment, but this time warm the hydrochloric acid in the conical flask to about 30 °C on a hotplate before adding the magnesium metal.

9. When the reaction is over, note the final volume of hydrogen collected, and then wash out the conical flask.

10. Repeat the experiment, but this time warm the hydrochloric acid in the conical flask to about 40 °C on a hotplate before adding the magnesium metal.

11. When the reaction is over, note the final volume of hydrogen collected, and then wash out the conical flask.

12. On the same sheet of graph paper, plot a graph of volume of hydrogen (y-axis) against time (x-axis) for each of the three experiments.

Student write-up

(i) Title of Experiment 21.6

_____

(ii) Date _____   Student _____

(iii) Equipment and chemicals used

_____

_____

_____

(iv) Procedure (outline what you did)

_____

_____

_____

_____

_____

(v) **Results**

Temperature 1 (room temperature) = _____

Temperature 2 (first heating) = _____

Temperature 3 (second heating) = _____

Time (s)										
Volume of H_2 (cm³) at room temperature										
Volume of H_2 (cm³) (first heating)										
Volume of H_2 (cm³) (second heating)										

Table L21.5

(vi) **Observations**

_____

_____

(vii) **Labelled diagram of apparatus**

(viii) **Conclusion**

_____

_____

Questions on this experiment can be found on folensonline.ie.

82   ESSENTIAL SCIENCE

Experiment 21.7

To investigate the effect of a catalyst on the rate of a reaction

Equipment required: conical flask, one-hole rubber stopper, glass tubing, rubber tubing, 100 cm³ graduated cylinder, 250 cm³ graduated cylinder, retort stand and clamp, stopclock, glass trough or plastic basin

Chemicals required: hydrogen peroxide (20 volume), manganese dioxide

Method

1. Using a 100 cm³ graduated cylinder, place 50 cm³ of 20 volume hydrogen peroxide in a conical flask.

2. Set up the apparatus shown in Fig. L21.7. The oxygen produced should be collected in a 250 cm³ graduated cylinder.

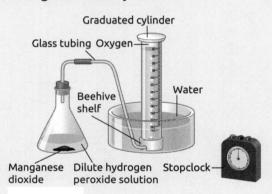

Fig. L21.7

3. Quickly add a small amount (enough to fit on the tip of a spatula) of manganese dioxide to the hydrogen peroxide in the conical flask. Immediately insert the stopper in the flask and start the stopclock. Give the conical flask a brief, gentle shake.

4. At regular intervals (e.g. every 10 seconds) record in Table L21.6 the volume of oxygen given off.

5. When the reaction is over, note the final volume of oxygen collected, and then wash out the conical flask into a large container. This ensures that the manganese dioxide is not wasted. The manganese dioxide can be filtered off, dried and used again.

6. Plot a graph of volume of oxygen (y-axis) against time (x-axis) on a sheet of graph paper.

Student write-up

(i) Title of Experiment 21.7

_____

(ii) Date _____ Student _____

(iii) Equipment and chemicals used

_____

_____

(iv) Procedure (outline what you did)

_____

_____

(v) Results

Time (min)									
Volume of O_2 (cm³)									

Table L21.6

(vi) Observations

_____

_____

(vii) Labelled diagram of apparatus

(viii) Conclusion

_____

Questions on this experiment may be found on folensonline.ie.

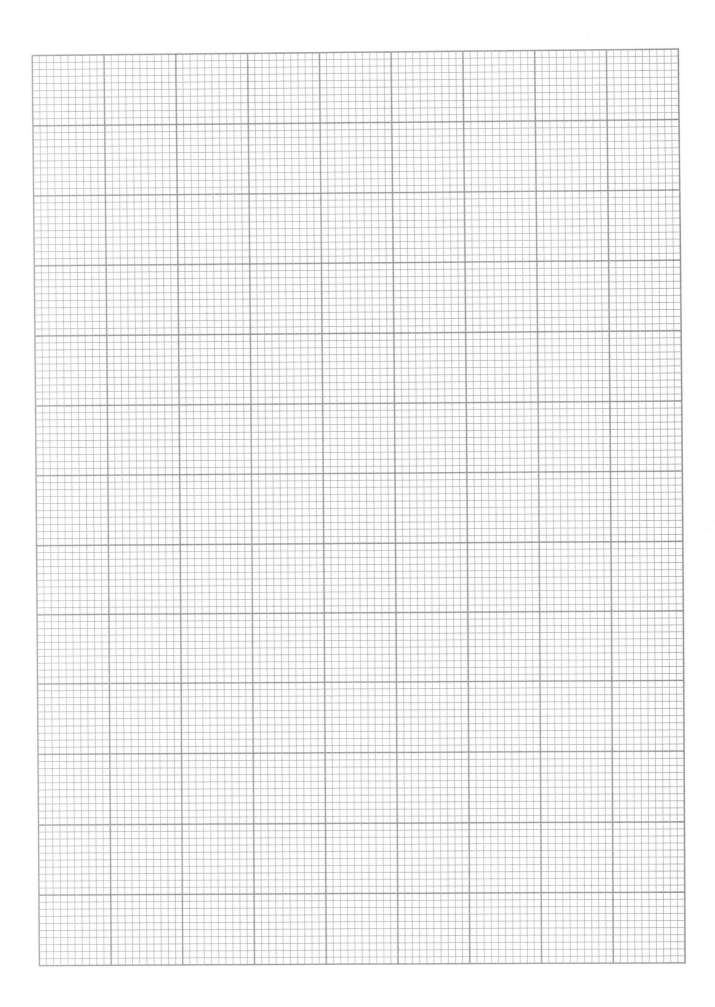

Experiment 22.1

To titrate hydrochloric acid (HCl) solution against sodium hydroxide (NaOH) solution and then to prepare a sample of sodium chloride (NaCl)

Equipment required: burette, conical flask, retort stand and clamp, pipette, pipette filler, white tile or white paper, funnel, wash bottle, dropper, evaporating dish, hotplate (or Bunsen burner, tripod and wire gauze), water bath or beaker

Chemicals required: dilute hydrochloric acid (1 M), dilute sodium hydroxide (1 M), methyl orange indicator

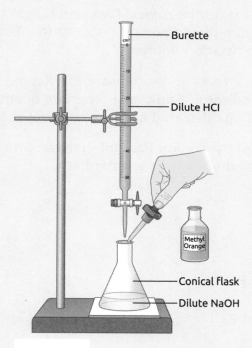

Fig. L22.1

Method

1. Set up the apparatus as shown in Fig. L22.1.

2. Rinse out a pipette with deionised water and with a small amount of the sodium hydroxide solution. Using the pipette filler and pipette, place 25 cm³ of the sodium hydroxide solution into a clean conical flask.

3. Wash out a burette with deionised water and also with a small amount of the hydrochloric acid solution. Use a funnel when pouring liquid into the burette.

4. Clamp the burette vertically in a retort stand and fill the burette to above the 0 cm³ mark with the hydrochloric acid solution. Open the tap to allow the part of the burette below the tap to fill. Adjust the bottom of the meniscus of the liquid to the 0 cm³ mark on the burette.

5. Add about three drops of methyl orange indicator to the conical flask.

6. Place a white tile or white paper under the conical flask. Allow the acid to run into the conical flask. Add about 2 cm³ of the acid at a time, swirling the conical flask continuously. Using the wash bottle of deionised water, wash down the sides of the conical flask from time to time.

7. When the red colour does not disappear almost immediately, add the acid a drop at a time until the colour remains slightly pink. Note the burette reading. This is the amount of acid solution required to neutralise 25 cm³ of sodium hydroxide solution. The conical flask now contains an almost neutral solution of sodium chloride, but it is coloured pink.

8. Wash out the contents of the conical flask and repeat the titration. The second titration figure should be fairly close to the first figure. Take the average of the two titration figures.

9. Again discard the contents of the conical flask. Repeat the experiment **without using an indicator**. Add the appropriate quantity of acid (i.e. the average value calculated above) to neutralise the alkali.

10. Pour the contents of the conical flask into an evaporating dish and evaporate almost to dryness over a water bath.

11. Leave the solution to cool.

Student write-up

(i) Title of Experiment 22.1

to titrate Hydrochloric acid against sodium hydroxide solution and then to prepare a sample of (Nacl)

(ii) Date 17 November   Student Abdul

(iii) Equipment and chemicals used

burgette, conical flask, retort stand and clamp, pipette filler, white tile, funnel, wash bottle, dropper, evaporating dish, hot plate water bath or breaker

(iv) Procedure (outline what you did)

add hydrochloric acid to solution to a known volume of sodium hydrochloric solution until a neutral solution is obtained you will then get a sample of salt from this neutral solution.

(v) Results and observations

White crystals are formed in the evaporating acid basin.

(vi) Labelled diagram of apparatus

(vii) Conclusion

hydrochloric and sodium hydroxide have reacted to form sodium chloride.

Questions on this experiment may be found on folensonline.ie.

LABORATORY NOTEBOOK   89

Student experiment 34

Experiment 26.1

To investigate the conditions necessary for rusting to occur

Equipment required: test tubes × 3, test-tube rack, rubber stopper, steel nails × 3

Chemicals required: calcium chloride, oil, water

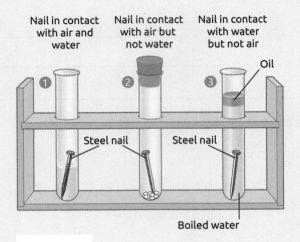

Fig. L26.1

Method

1. Set up three test tubes, as shown in Fig. L26.1.

2. Place a nail in test tube 1. This test tube contains both air and water.

3. Place a second nail in test tube 2, which contains some calcium chloride. Calcium chloride is a substance that absorbs water. Therefore, there is no water in the air in test tube 2. Stopper the test tube to prevent moisture from the air getting in.

4. Place a third nail in test tube 3, which contains some boiled water. While the water is still hot, cover the water with some oil. This prevents any air dissolving in the water when the water cools down.

5. Leave the apparatus to stand for a few days.

6. Write down your observation.

Student write-up

(i) Title of Experiment 26.1

_____

(ii) Date _____   Student _____

(iii) Equipment and chemicals (reagent) used

_____

_____

(iv) Procedure (outline what you did)

_____

_____

_____

_____

(v) Results and observations

_____

_____

(vi) Labelled diagram of apparatus

(vii) Conclusion

_____

Questions on this experiment may be found on folensonline.ie.

LABORATORY NOTEBOOK   91

Experiment 29.1
To find the density of a regular solid

Introduction

In this experiment you will find the mass and the volume of a rectangular block and hence calculate its density.

Equipment required: rectangular block, electronic balance, ruler, graduated cylinder

Chemicals required: various liquids such as water, sunflower oil, etc.

Method

1. Place the block on an electronic balance and note its mass.

2. Using a ruler, find the length, width and height of the block.

Calculations

1. Calculate the volume of the cube: Volume = length × width × height

2. Divide the mass of the block by the volume. This gives you the density. Do not forget to write the units with your answer.

Fig. L29.1

Student write-up

(i) Title of Experiment 29.1

_____

(ii) Date _____   Student _____

(iii) Equipment used _____

_____

(iv) Procedure (outline what you did)

_____

_____

_____

(iv) Results

Mass of block   = _____ g

Length (*l*)   = _____ cm

Width (*w*)   = _____ cm

Height (*h*)   = _____ cm

Volume (*V*)   = _____ cm³ $V = l \times w \times h$

Density = mass/volume   = _____ **g/cm³**

(vi) Labelled diagram of apparatus

(vii) Conclusion

_____

Questions on this experiment can be found on folensonline.ie.

Experiment 29.2

To find the density of an irregular-shaped object

Introduction

In this experiment you will find the mass and the volume of a stone and hence calculate its density.

Equipment required: overflow can, graduated cylinder (250 cm³), string, stone or potato, electronic balance

Method

1. Find the mass of a dry stone by placing it on a balance.

2. Tie a piece of string around the stone.

3. Fill an overflow can as much as possible with water, at the edge of the sink with the spout pointing into the sink.

4. Place a graduated cylinder under the spout of the overflow can.

5. Ask a friend to gently lower the stone into the can of water. Water will flow from the overflow can into the graduated cylinder. Wait until the water stops flowing out of the can.

6. Place the graduated cylinder on the bench and read the volume of water inside. (Remember: read the bottom of the meniscus at eye level!)

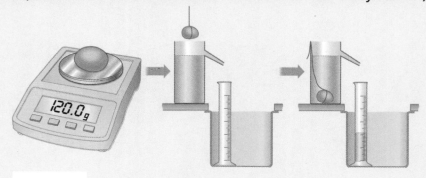

Fig. L29.2

Calculations

Divide the mass of the stone by the volume of water. You have now calculated the density.

Student write-up

(i) Title of Experiment 29.2

_____

(ii) Date _____ Student _____

(iii) Equipment used _____

_____

(iv) Procedure (outline what you did)

_____

_____

_____

_____

(v) Results

Mass of block (*m*)   = _____ g

Volume (*V*)   = _____ cm³

Density = mass/volume = _____ g/cm³

(vi) Labelled diagram of apparatus

(vii) Conclusion

_____

Questions on this experiment can be found on folensonline.ie.

LABORATORY NOTEBOOK   95

Experiment 29.3
To find the density of a liquid

Introduction

In this experiment you will find the mass and the volume of a liquid and hence calculate its density.

Equipment required: beaker, electronic balance

Method

Fig. L29.3

1. Using a graduated cylinder measure out a volume of 50 cm³ of a liquid.

2. Place a clean dry beaker on an electronic balance and write down its mass.

3. Pour the liquid into the beaker and find the mass of the beaker and liquid.

Calculations

1. Find the mass of the liquid by subtracting the mass of the empty beaker from the mass of the beaker and liquid.

2. Divide the mass of the liquid by the volume of the liquid. This gives you the density.

Student write-up

(i) Title of Experiment 29.3

_____

(ii) Date _____   Student _____

(iii) Equipment used

_____

_____

(iv) Procedure (outline what you did)

_____

_____

_____

(v) Results

Mass of empty beaker   = _____ g

Mass of beaker and liquid = _____ g

Mass of liquid (*m*)   = _____ g

Volume of liquid (*V*)   = _____ cm³

Density = mass/volume   = _____ g/cm³

(vi) Labelled diagram of apparatus

(vii) Conclusion

_____

Questions on this experiment can be found on folensonline.ie.

LABORATORY NOTEBOOK   97

Experiment 30.1

To use a data logger to measure the speed of an object

Introduction

In this experiment you will measure the speed of an object using a data logger.

Equipment required: track, trolley, motion sensor with computer or data logger

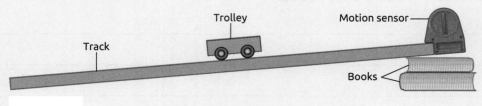

Trolley

Track

Motion sensor

Books

Fig. L30.1

Method

1. Place a trolley on a track. Adjust the slope so that the trolley runs with a constant speed after being given a gentle push.

2. Connect a motion sensor to a computer or data logger. Ensure that the switch on the motion sensor is set to 'trolley'.

3. Set the data-logging software to plot a graph of distance against time.

4. Place the trolley in front of the motion sensor on the track.

5. Give the trolley a gentle push. As soon as you remove your hand from the trolley, click 'start'. You may need to ask a classmate to help you. Ensure that your hand does not get in front of the motion sensor. When the trolley gets to the bottom of the track, click on 'stop'.

6. Analyse the graph using the slope tool. The slope of the graph is the speed of the car.

7. Repeat the experiment, but this time give the trolley a slightly harder push.

   Note that if the graph produced is not a straight line, the trolley is not moving at constant velocity. The slope of the track will need to be adjusted.

Student write-up

(i) Title of Experiment 30.1

_____

(ii) Date _____ Student _____

(iii) Equipment used

_____

_____

(iv) Procedure (outline what you did)

_____

_____

_____

(v) Results and observations

_____

_____

_____

(vi) Labelled diagram of apparatus

(vii) Conclusion

_____

_____

Questions on this experiment may be found on folensonline.ie.

Student experiment 39

Experiment 30.2

To use a data logger to measure the acceleration of an object

Introduction

In this experiment you will measure the acceleration of an object using a data logger.

Equipment required: track, trolley, motion sensor with computer or data logger

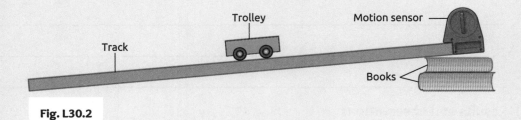

Trolley

Motion sensor

Track

Books

Fig. L30.2

Method

1. Place a trolley on a track. Adjust the slope so that the trolley gradually gets faster as it travels down the track, i.e. it accelerates as it moves down the track.

2. Connect a motion sensor to a computer or data logger. Ensure that the switch on the motion sensor is set to 'trolley'.

3. Set the data-logging software to plot a graph of velocity/time.

4. Place the trolley in front of the motion sensor on the track. A friend may have to hold the trolley from the side to keep it in place. Be prepared to catch the trolley at the end of the next step.

5. Let the trolley go. As soon as you remove your hand from the trolley, click 'start'. You may need to ask a classmate to help you. Ensure that your hand does not get in front of the motion sensor.

6. When the trolley gets to the bottom of the track click on 'stop'.

7. Find the slope of the graph using the slope tool in the software. This should tell you the acceleration of the trolley.

8. Repeat the experiment using a slightly steeper slope on the track.

Student write-up

(i) Title of Experiment 30.2

_____

(ii) Date _____ **Student** _____

(iii) Equipment used

_____

_____

(iv) Procedure (outline what you did)

_____

_____

_____

(v) Results and observations

_____

_____

_____

(vi) Labelled diagram of apparatus

(vii) Conclusion

_____

_____

Questions on this experiment may be found on folensonline.ie.

Student experiment 40

Experiment 31.1

To investigate the relationship between the extension of a spiral spring and the force applied to it

Equipment required: spiral spring, metre stick or ruler, retort stand with 2 clamps, slotted weights and holder with pointer attached

Method

1. Set up the apparatus as shown in Fig. L31.1. Hang the spiral spring from a clamp. Hang the weight holder from the bottom of the spring.

2. In a separate clamp adjust the metre stick vertically until the pointer from the weight hanger is pointing directly at the zero mark. It may be easier to use a ruler.

3. Add a weight to the weight holder. Note the length and the weight added.

4. Add more weights one by one, noting the total added weight and the total extension.

Note 1

If you overstretch a spring it will be damaged. A spring may be stretched a certain amount **(the elastic limit)** before it will be damaged. Your teacher will have matched the spring to the weights used.

Note 2

If you are unable to get the pointer to point to the zero mark at the beginning of the experiment, note the position of the pointer before any weights are added. Then note the position as each weight is added. The extension can be found by subtraction.

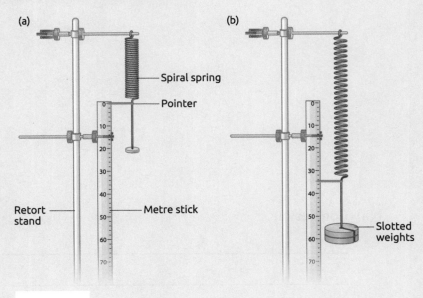

Fig. L31.1

Student write-up

(i) Title of Experiment 31.1

_____

(ii) Date _____   Student _____

(iii) Equipment used

_____

(iv) Procedure (outline what you did)

_____

_____

_____

(v) Labelled diagram of apparatus

(vi) Results and observations

Force (N)	0					
Length (cm)						
Extension (cm)						

(vii) Conclusion

_____

Questions on this experiment may be found on folensonline.ie.

LABORATORY NOTEBOOK   103

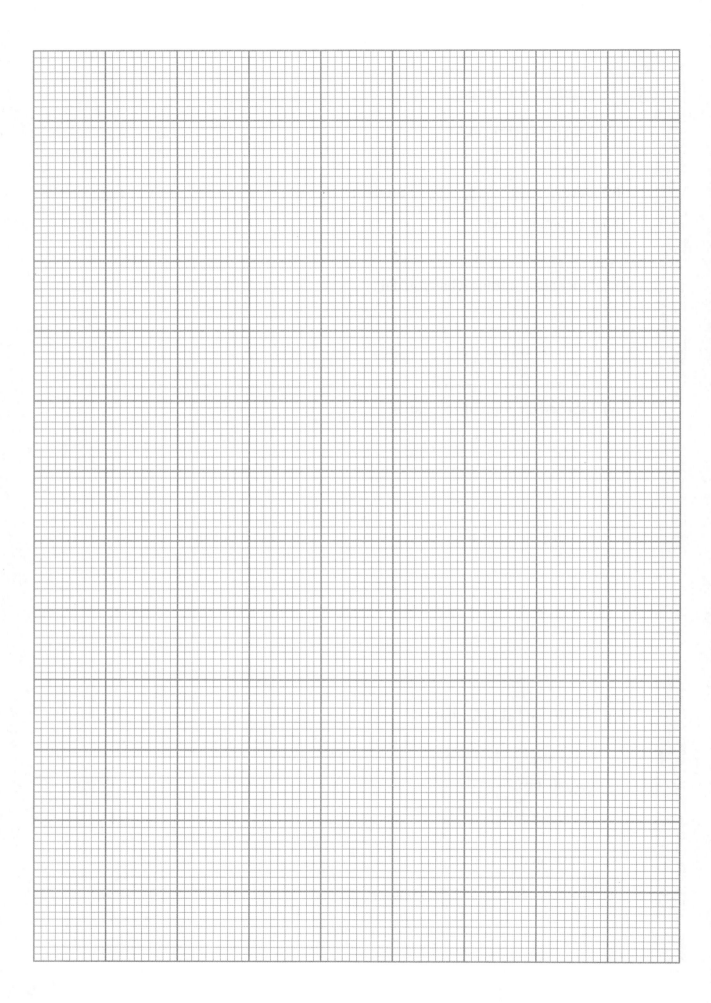

Experiment 32.1

To build and test a device that transforms energy from one form to another in order to perform a function; to describe the energy changes and ways of improving efficiency

Introduction

In this experiment you will investigate the factors that affect the efficiency of a motor connected to a solar panel.

Equipment required: solar panel, motor, fan

Method

1. Construct the circuit shown in Fig. L32.1. It consists of a solar panel connected to a motor, which has a fan connected.

2. Expose the solar panel to light. Observe the speed of the motor.

3. Carry out various adjustments, such as light source, distance between light source and solar panel, and angle of panel with light, to improve the efficiency of the solar panel.

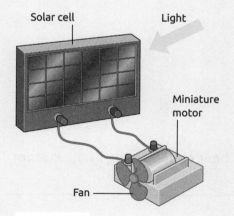

Fig. L32.1

Student write-up

(i) **Title of Experiment 32.1**

_____

(ii) **Date** _____ **Student** _____

(iii) **Equipment used**

_____

_____

(iv) **Procedure (outline what you did)**

_____

_____

_____

(v) **Results and observations**

_____

_____

(vi) **Labelled diagram of apparatus**

(vii) **Describe the energy changes happening in the system**

_____

_____

(viii) **How the efficiency of the system can be improved**

_____

_____

Questions on this experiment may be found on folensonline.ie.

106   ESSENTIAL SCIENCE

Student experiment 42

Experiment 33.1

To show transfer of heat energy by conduction and to investigate the rate of conduction in different metals

Introduction

In this experiment you will investigate conduction in different metals.

Equipment required: conduction in metals apparatus, Vaseline, timer, tacks or matchsticks

Method

1. Place an equal amount (a small blob) of Vaseline at the end of the metal rods.

2. Connect a blunt tack or matchstick to each rod.

3. Place some hot water in the tank of the apparatus as shown in the diagram.

4. Note the time it takes for each tack or matchstick to fall off each rod.

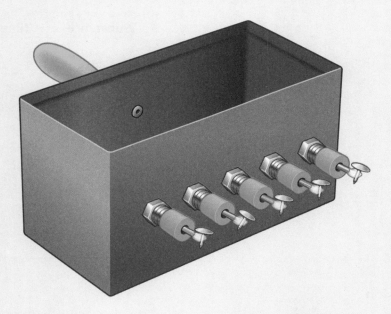

Fig. L33.1

Student write-up

(i) Title of Experiment 33.1

investigate conduction in different metals

(ii) Date 9/January **Student** _____

(iii) Equipment used

appartus, vaseline, timer, match sticks

_____

(iv) Procedure (outline what you did)

Place equal amounts of vaseline on end of metal rods,
connect matchstick to rods, Place hot water in
tank, note the time to see what material fall
quicker

(v) Results and observations

_____

_____

(vi) Labelled diagram of apparatus

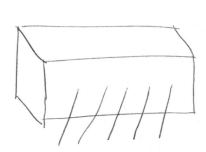

Substance	Time to fall
Alaminium	
Steel	

(vii) Conclusion

the match sticks which falls faster adects
the best conductor results.

Questions on this experiment may be found on folensonline.ie.

ESSENTIAL SCIENCE

Experiment 33.2

To show convection currents in a liquid

Introduction

In this experiment you will show convection currents in a liquid.

Equipment required: round-bottomed flask, straight drinking straw, Bunsen burner, retort stand, pipette or forceps

Chemicals required: dye such as potassium permanganate

Method

1. Place a crystal of dye at the bottom of a round-bottomed flask using a forceps and a straw (for fine crystals it might be possible to use a disposable pipette instead of forceps).

2. Heat the water in the flask gently using a Bunsen burner. Note your observations.

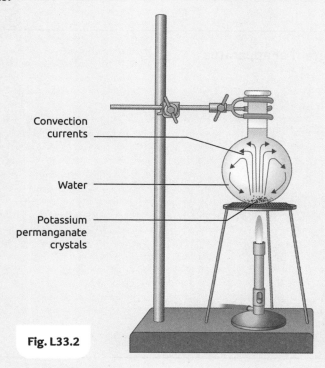

Convection currents

Water

Potassium permanganate crystals

Fig. L33.2

Student write-up

(i) Title of Experiment 33.2

_____

(ii) Date _____   Student _____

(iii) Equipment used

_____

_____

(iv) Procedure (outline what you did)

_____

_____

_____

(v) Results and observations

_____

_____

_____

(vi) Labelled diagram of apparatus

(vii) Conclusions

_____

_____

Questions on this experiment may be found on folensonline.ie.

ESSENTIAL SCIENCE

Experiment 33.3
To show convection currents in air

Introduction

In this experiment you will show convection currents in air.

Equipment required: convection in air apparatus, candle, paper, matches

Method

1. Light a candle and place it under one of the chimneys in the apparatus as shown in Fig. L33.3.

2. Close the front glass door as much as possible.

3. Place a smouldering piece of paper over the other chimney of the apparatus to observe the movement of air around the apparatus. Note what you observe.

Fig. L33.3

Student write-up

(i) Title of Experiment 33.3

_____

(ii) Date _____   **Student** _____

(iii) Equipment used

_____

_____

(iv) Procedure (outline what you did)

_____

_____

_____

(v) Results and observations

_____

_____

_____

(vi) Labelled diagram of apparatus

(vii) Conclusion

_____

_____

Questions on this experiment may be found on folensonline.ie.

Experiment 33.4

To investigate heat transfer by radiation

Introduction

In this experiment you will investigate heat transfer by radiation.

Equipment required: black can, similar white or shiny can, thermometers × 2

Method

1. Place equal volumes of hot water at the same temperature in two cans made of the same material.

2. Note the temperature of both cans every 5 minutes.

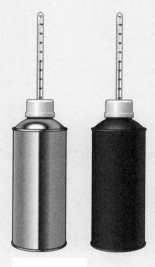

Fig. L33.4

Student write-up

(i) Title of Experiment 33.4

_____

(ii) Date _____ Student _____

(iii) Equipment used

_____

(iv) Procedure (outline what you did)

_____

_____

(v) Results and observations

Time (minutes)	Temperature of white or shiny can (°C)	Temperature of black can (°C)
5		
10		
15		
20		
25		
30		

(vi) Draw a graph of temperature against time, placing both sets of results on the same graph.

(vii) Labelled diagram of apparatus

(viii) Conclusion

_____

Questions on this experiment may be found on folensonline.ie.

114   ESSENTIAL SCIENCE

Experiment 34.1

To classify materials as electrical conductors or insulators

Introduction

In this experiment you will investigate different substances to determine whether they are electrical conductors or insulators.

Equipment required: battery, bulb with holder, wires, crocodile clips, materials to be tested such as wood, coins, paperclips, biro, rubber band, ruler and pencil 'lead' (graphite)

Method

1. Set up the apparatus as shown in Fig. L34.1.

2. Connect the two crocodile clips together to ensure that the bulb is working.

3. Place different substances between the crocodile clips and note if the bulb lights or not.

4. Tabulate your results.

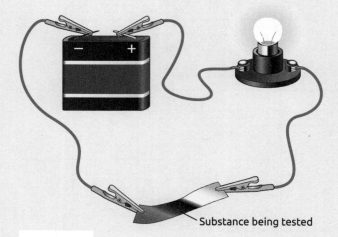

Substance being tested

Fig. L34.1

Student write-up

(i) Title of Experiment 34.1

_____

(ii) Date _____   Student _____

(iii) Equipment used _____

_____

(iv) Procedure (outline what you did) _____

_____

_____

(v) Results and observations _____

Substance	Observation: does the bulb light?	Conclusion: conductor/insulator?

(vi) Labelled diagram of apparatus

(vii) Conclusion

_____

Questions on this experiment may be found on folensonline.ie.

LABORATORY NOTEBOOK   117

Student experiment 47

Experiment 34.2

To investigate how the current flowing in a conductor varies with voltage and to determine the resistance of the conductor

Introduction

In this experiment you will find out how current across a conductor varies with voltage and how to determine the resistance of the conductor.

Equipment required: resistance wire, connecting leads × 5, crocodile clips × 4, ammeter, voltmeter, variable resistor, 6 volt battery

Method

1. Connect the ammeter, the battery, the resistance wire and a variable resistor in series with each other as shown in Fig. L34.2.

2. Add the voltmeter in parallel across the resistance wire as shown in Fig. L34.3.

3. Adjust the sliding contact of the variable resistor to give as low a voltage reading as possible (e.g. 0.5 V). Note the corresponding current.

4. Adjust the sliding contact on the variable resistor to give a higher voltage reading (1.0 V) and note the current.

5. Repeat step 4 at least another four times and note the current flowing when a higher voltage is applied.

6. Tabulate your results.

7. Draw a graph of voltage versus current.

8. Using the formula $R = \dfrac{V}{I}$ find the resistance of the wire using a value of voltage and its corresponding current.

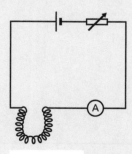

Fig. L34.2

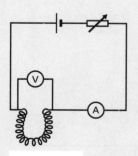

Fig. L34.3

Student write-up

(i)   Title of Experiment 34.2

_____

(ii) Date _____   Student _____

(iii) Equipment used

_____

_____

_____

(iv) Procedure (outline what you did)

_____

_____

_____

_____

_____

_____

_____

_____

(v)   Results and observations

_____

_____

_____

Voltage (V)	Current (A)

(vi) Labelled diagram of apparatus

(vii) Conclusions

_____

_____

_____

_____

Questions on this experiment may be found on folensonline.ie.

120   ESSENTIAL SCIENCE

Experiment 34.3

To investigate the operation of a diode

Introduction

In this experiment you will find out about the operation of a diode.

Equipment required: diode, mounted bulb, battery, connecting leads × 4, switch

Method

1. Set up the circuit as shown in Fig. L34.4. Ensure that the negative side of the diode faces the negative side of the battery. Turn on the switch and observe what happens.

2. Reverse the diode in the circuit as in Fig. L34.5.

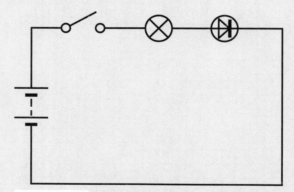

Fig. L34.4

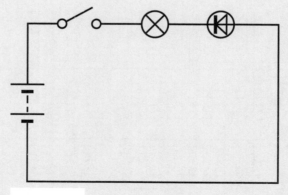

Fig. L34.5

Student write-up

(i) Title of Experiment 34.3

_____

(ii) Date _____   **Student** _____

(iii) Equipment used _____

_____

(iv) Procedure (outline what you did)

_____

_____

_____

_____

(v) Results and observations

_____

_____

(vi) Labelled diagram of apparatus

(vii) Conclusion

_____

_____

Questions on this experiment may be found on folensonline.ie.

Student experiment 49

Experiment 34.4
To investigate the operation of a light-emitting diode

Introduction

In this experiment you will find out about the operation of a light-emitting diode (LED).

Equipment required: light-emitting diodes × 2, battery, connecting leads × 7, switch, 330 Ω resistor

Method

Set up the circuit shown in Fig. L34.6, consisting of two LEDs connected to a battery and a resistor. Note that the diodes are in parallel but in opposite directions.

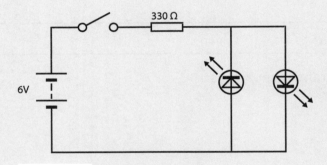

Fig. L34.6

 ### Student write-up

(i) Title of Experiment 34.4

_____

(ii) Date _____ Student _____

(iii) Equipment used _____

_____

_____

(iv) Procedure (outline what you did)

_____

_____

_____

(v) Results and observations

_____

_____

_____

_____

(vi) Labelled diagram of apparatus

(vii) Conclusion

_____

_____

_____

_____

Questions on this experiment may be found on folensonline.ie.

Experiment 34.5

To investigate the operation of a light-dependent resistor

Introduction

In this experiment you will find out about the operation of a light-dependent resistor (LDR).

Equipment required: light-dependent resistor, buzzer, battery, connecting leads × 3, light source

Method

1. Set up the apparatus as shown in Fig. L34.7.

2. Close the switch. Note what you observe.

3. Place a bright light closer to the LDR. Note what you observe.

4. Place a finger over the LDR. Note what you observe.

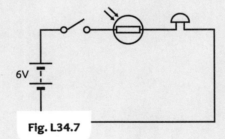

6V

Fig. L34.7

Student write-up

(i) Title of Experiment 34.5

_____

(ii) Date _____ Student _____

(iii) Equipment used _____

_____

(iv) Procedure (outline what you did)

_____

_____

_____

_____

(v) Results and observations

_____

_____

(vi) Labelled diagram of apparatus

(vii) Conclusion

_____

_____

Questions on this experiment may be found on folensonline.ie.

Experiment 34.6

To investigate the operation of a thermistor

Introduction

In this experiment you will find out how the resistance of a thermistor changes with temperature.

Equipment required: thermistor, battery, connecting leads × 7, switch, buzzer

Method

1. Set up the apparatus as shown in Fig. L34.8.

2. Close the switch. Note what you observe.

3. Place the thermistor in a small beaker of hot water. Note what you observe.

4. Now place the thermistor in cold water. What do you observe?

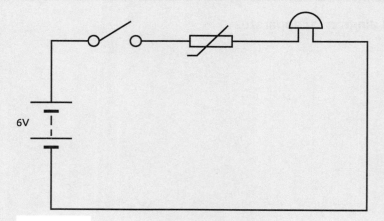

Fig. L34.8

Student write-up

(i) Title of Experiment 34.6

_____

(ii) Date _____   Student _____

(iii) Equipment used _____

_____

(iv) Procedure (outline what you did)

_____

_____

_____

_____

(v) Results and observations

_____

_____

(vi) Labelled diagram of apparatus

(vii) Conclusion

_____

_____

Questions on this experiment may be found on folensonline.ie.